1001
IMAGES OF
CARS

TEXT BY JÉROME BUREAU

CRESCENT BOOKS
NEW YORK • AVENEL, NEW JERSEY

CONTENTS

CLB 2895
© 1993 Colour Library Books Ltd., Godalming, Surrey, England
All rights reserved
This 1993 edition published by Crescent Books
distributed by Outlet Book Company, Inc.
a Random House Company
40 Engelhard Avenue, Avenel, New Jersey 07001
Printed and bound in Malaysia.
ISBN 0 517 06944 X
8 7 6 5 4 3 2 1

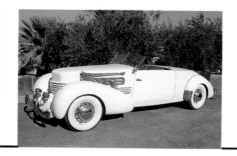

FOREWORD

C liché though it may be, how can one avoid stating the obvious: the motor car is both symbol and icon of the twentieth century. Although its origins can, in theory, be traced back over two hundred years to the first steam carriage of Nicolas Cugnot, the 1990s are in fact a far more appropriate time for celebrating the centenary of its invention.

The brilliant, somewhat madcap engineers who with their own hands put together the first models in improvised workshops could never have imagined that, a century later, tens of millions of automobiles a year would be pouring off production lines in countries all round the world. A few of the most famous marques – Ford, Renault, Fiat and Rover – are still around to bear witness to this amazing chapter in human history.

It is not without reason that the twentieth century has been called the age of the motor car. Symbol of freedom before it came to be seen as the new monster roaming the urban jungle, inexhaustible laboratory of technical innovations, object of constant artistic research, though a part of everyone's daily life, the motor car has continued to be a source of dreams. And while one may make fun of the exaggerated affection with which individuals regard their car, one cannot help noticing that people also keep a hallowed place in their hearts for the car they aspire to own one day: the car of their dreams. Maybe you will find such a car in the pages of this book, among superb American monsters of the 1930s, eternally seductive British or Italian sports cars, magnificent models of French or German extraction ….

The motor car has become on the one hand a museum piece, on the other the indispensable tool of modern living, a commonplace object and a rarity. Even 1001 photographs will not suffice to tell the full story of the most prolific (and in many ways the most significant) of modern industries, but we have striven to include all the important models, those which characterized their period, and those which still keep up the old traditions.

The automobile has always had to face up to four more or less contradictory imperatives: solidity, beauty, speed and usefulness. These will be the cardinal points of our compass as we take a drive through the century of the motor car.

THE ALL-TIME GREATS

MODEL T FORD • LANCIA LAMBDA • AUSTIN SEVEN

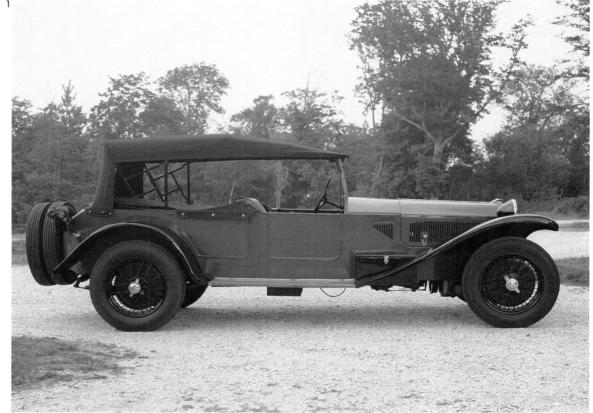

The **Model T Ford** was the first standard model in automobile history, the first mass-produced vehicle, the first popular car. It was designed by J. Galand and H.J. Wills, just five years after Henry Ford had launched his company. To quote a famous phrase, the Model T "put America on four wheels", ushering a predominantly rural society into the twentieth century. Tough, reliable and reasonably priced ($850) for its time, when launched in 1908, the four-seater was the first car to be manufactured by F.W. Taylor's assembly-line methods. This made it possible to cut production time from twelve hours to little more than one hour per car! Ford sold more than fifteen million Model Ts in the years 1908 to 1927, a record bettered only by Volkswagen in later years. The high point was 1923, when more than two million of the cars were produced. Thereafter, it went into decline as the road network began to improve. Its famed robustness and manoeuvrability had proved equal to all obstacles.

The **Lancia Lambda** will be remembered as the masterpiece of Vincenzo Lancia, who first presented it at the Paris and London Motor Shows in 1922. It was revolutionary in design, the integral body and frame not requiring the support of a separate chassis. Between 1922 and 1931, twelve thousand of the cars were produced, in eight series. The 1931 model was particularly sporty, reaching a top speed of 81 mph.

The **Austin Seven** was the first people's car, designed by Herbert Austin himself. Unveiled at the 1922 London Motor Show, the car was so well liked that it continued in production without any significant modifications until 1939. Austin had intended that it should be a true family car, with two seats for children at the rear, despite its modest dimensions and pocket-sized engine (696 cc in the case of the standard model). Costing less than £200, in the late 1920s it held more than a two-thirds share of the British car market. Over 300,000 of the cars were sold before they were superseded by the Austin Ten and the Big Seven.

6

8

12

9

13

Model T Ford

1911 model (8); 1914 model (9); 1915 model (7 and 13, close up of the radiator and headlights); 1923 model (12); view of the factory (10).

Lancia Lambda

1928 model, with close-up of engine (1 and 4); 1930 model (2).

Austin Seven

1923 model (5); 1929 model (3); rear view of Swallow version (11); head-on view of 1937 model (6).

PREVIOUS PAGES: E-Type Jaguar, with insets of the Porsche 911 and the Mercedes 300 SL, three of the great sports cars.

7

10

11

MINI • VOLKSWAGEN • GOLF

The **Mini** – a name covering several very similar models produced by the merged Austin and Morris companies – is undoubtedly one of the most amazing cars ever manufactured. The Morris company was founded at the beginning of the century by Richard Morris, who began his career repairing bicycles and rose to become Lord Nuffield. In 1951, his company merged with Austin to form the British Motor Corporation (BMC), though the separate Austin and Morris names were retained. The most famous child of this marriage was the Mini, or Morris Mini-Minor, which made its debut in 1959. Its many versions have been strong contenders in the car market ever since. Designed by the brilliant engineer Alec Issigonis, this small car was ideal for the new urban conditions and, in its legendary "S" version, it enjoyed sparkling success in rallying.

Volkswagen means "people's car". The make and concept were willed by the Nazi regime, which was behind its development in 1937. Almost immediately, the new company launched a tough, compact and deliberately modest car, which its designer, the brilliant Ferdinand Porsche, then 63 years of age, baptized *Kraft durch Freude* (KDF), meaning "strength through joy". Nowadays, of course, it is known only by its pet name of Beetle; the car given wings by Walt Disney. In 1972, the Volkswagen beat the production record previously held by the Model T Ford (fifteen million units), eventually going on to achieve production figures of twenty-one million! Although its original 985cc engine evolved over the years and technical progress brought modifications to mechanical components, its characteristic silhouette remained the same, eternally rotund and friendly. Only a few Beetles are produced today.

The **Golf** was unveiled in 1974, Volkswagen at last breaking its one-car tradition and marketing three new models: the Passat, the Scirocco and the Golf. And it was the Golf, with its more crafted bodywork (by the Italian Giorgetto Giugiaro), excellent performance and handling (especially with the appearance of the GTI version in 1976), and dimensions better suited to modern driving conditions, which has proved an enduring success. The third version of the Golf is now in production, the German manufacturer having sold over fourteen million of the cars since 1974.

The Mini

A 1959 example of the Austin Mini Seven (5); the Mini Cooper S, 1964 (4); an exhibition of Minis, 1980 (1); and the engine of a 1981 Austin Mini 1000HL (2).

The Volkswagen

First there was the 1938 KDF (7), to be followed by over twenty million of its kind, including these three 1947 models (6, 9 and 10).

The Golf

Three equally successful versions, 1974, 1981 and 1983 (3); a 1989 version of the sporty GTI (8).

CITROEN • RENAULT • PEUGEOT

André **Citroën** will undoubtedly be remembered as one of the most brilliant automobile engineers of the first half of the century. No car proves it better than the glorious "Traction", whose 7 hp version was first introduced in 1934, to be joined a few months later by a more powerful 11 hp model. It is almost impossible to convey just how revolutionary a car it was, incorporating front-wheel drive, independent suspension, integral steel body, all-round hydraulic brakes and other daring innovations. The Traction's career was to last almost twenty-four years, though not as long as the inimitable 2 CV, which would have made its appearance in the late 1930s but for the war. Ideally suited to the explosion in car ownership, very reasonably priced, and extremely robust and manoeuvrable, the 2 CV eventually made its debut at the 1948 Paris Motor Show. In 1955, Citroën again revolutionized automobile design with the DS 19 (followed by the 21), which set new standards in suspension, gearbox and clutch technology. Traction, 2 CV and DS: a fabulous trio.

Peugeot has been producing cars for over a hundred years, some of which we shall be examining at a later stage. For this chapter devoted to legendary cars, we have chosen one of the marque's latest creations, the 205, which was launched in 1983. The success in rallying of the 205 Turbo 16 version guaranteed the car's success and contributed to the renaissance of this prestigious French firm.

In 1945 **Renault** made a new start as a nationalized company, forty-seven years after its foundation by Louis Renault and the appearance of its first small car. Few then believed in the company's future, or in the future of its new model, the 4 CV, the plans for which the new boss, Pierre Lefacheux, had found tucked away in a box of drawings. Unveiled at the 1946 Paris Motor Show, the small, rear-wheel-drive car with the 760cc engine was in fact to lead Renault's recovery and inaugurate an enviable tradition. It was followed by the R4, a 4 hp car with front-wheel drive, introduced in 1961, and much later by the R5. Today, the latest Renault, the Clio, is still France's best-selling motor car.

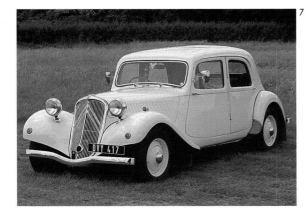

Citroën

Three examples of the Traction, in 7 hp (7 and 8) and 11 hp (9) versions; the DS21 (2), and its cabriolet version (1 and 4); a 1980 model of the 2 CV (6).

Peugeot

The 205 Turbo (10).

Renault

The 4 CV, 1955 (11); the Renault 4, popularly known as the 4L (5); and the Renault 5 (3).

FERRARI 250 GT • JAGUAR E-TYPE ALFA GIULIETTA PORSCHE 911 MERCEDES 300 SL • BMW 507

These six models are like six heartbeats, six all-too-brief stages in the dashing history of sports car development. The choice is inevitably partial, but stresses the vital importance of the six marques represented here.

In the front rank is, of course, **Ferrari**, symbolized by the prancing horse. Enzo Ferrari, a man of genius, set up his firm after gaining experience with his own racing team. Almost all his models have been outstanding, but the 250 GT range, introduced in the early 1960s, best symbolizes the firm's reputation for aesthetic perfection and state-of-the-art engineering.

A similar legend attaches to the **E-Type Jaguar**, introduced in 1961, a worthy successor to the famous XK 120. Despite its elongated bonnet, futuristic lines and brilliant performance (top speed in excess of 156 mph), the price was not out of the way for a sports car of such class, and it met with enormous success.

Another highly successful sports car was the **Mercedes 300SL**, unquestionably the finest model ever designed by the German firm. Unveiled in 1952 as an experimental car with "gull-wing" doors and a three-litre, six-cylinder engine, it put Mercedes back on the winning trail, achieving victory at Le Mans in 1953.

Another great German car, the **BMW 507** (with its younger sisters, the 501 and the 503), gave this marque its place among the top sports car manufacturers. The story began with the 328, one of the famous cabriolets of pre-war days. The 507 continued the tradition, even though only 250 of the cars existed when production ceased in the late 1950s.

The **Porsche 911**, introduced in 1946, worthily represents the quality we have come to expect of the Stuttgart firm. The spirit of Ferdinand Porsche lives on.

For four decades, from the 1950s to the 1980s, the Giulietta was the standard bearer of the great Alfa Romeo marque. Mechanically and aesthetically, it represented the best traditions of Italian automobile engineering.

Six sports cars, six moments from the past, six occasions to dream.

7

10

14

11

15

Ferrari

The 250 GT Berlinetta Lusso (1); a racing version (7); a model entered for the 1959 Tour de France (10).

Jaguar

The E-Type roadster, 1963, and close-up of headlight and bodywork (2 and 5); an E-Type Series II (3).

Mercedes

The gull-wing 300 SL (1 and 15).

Porsche

A 1965 911 S (14); a 1987 911 Turbo Sport (9).

BMW

The 507 and 503 series (8); a 1958 model of the 507 (12); and the more recent (1985) 318 (13).

Alfa Romeo

A recent version of the Giulietta (1981), and a view of the engine compartment (4 and 6).

8

12

9

13

THE PIONEERS

BENZ • FIAT • FORD • RENAULT
MERCER • PANHARD
CITROEN • BERLIET

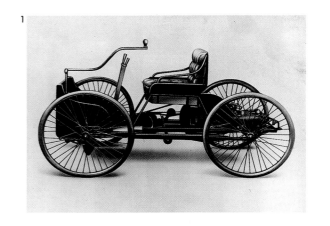

The first functioning automobile was a self-propelled steam tractor for hauling artillery built in 1796 by the French engineer Nicolas Cugnot, who had left the army to pursue his madcap projects at the court of Francis I in Vienna. However, the birth of the motor car as we know it dates from the end of the last century, when, on 29 January 1886, the German engineer Karl Benz patented a gas-powered tricycle or "velocipede". Not long before, Gottlieb Daimler had experimented with a two-wheeler powered by a four-stroke engine. Despite these undeniable German advances, it was in France, in 1890, that the first modern automobile saw the light of day: a four-wheel vehicle driven by petrol rather than steam, designed by Emile Levassor. The Frenchman set up the firm of **Panhard** and Levassor after marrying the widow of Edouard Sarrazin, founder of the Panhard company. In 1891, a prototype performed a tremendous feat, covering the twenty kilometres from Ivry in the east of Paris to Le Point du Jour in the west without stopping. Panhard and Levassor were also the first firm to manufacture automobiles on any scale, while other makes such as **Renault**, **Berliet**, Delahaye and **Fiat** began to develop, and Benz and Daimler finally produced viable motor cars.

Some unforgettable machines were manufactured during these feverish early years: the Panhard Phénix of 1895 (in which Emile Levassor met his death while racing); Louis Renault's first "voiturettes" of 1898, and the famous taxis which, in 1914, tipped the scales in the Battle of the Marne; the first cars produced by the Fabbrica Italiana Automobili Torino (FIAT for short), set up by Giovanni Agnelli in 1899; or the model "A" designed by Henry **Ford** in his workshops in Detroit. Finally, there were the legendary **Mercers**. This American company, founded in 1911, produced the first true sports cars, in particular the famous 35 Raceabout, a thoroughbred years in advance of its time. Like Panhard, which was later absorbed by **Citroën**, Mercer was not destined to endure, going out of business in the 1930s. By then, the car industry was fully fledged, and giants of the calibre of Renault, Fiat and Ford are still producing cars today.

Ford

The experimental model designed by Henry Ford in 1896 (1 and 6); though capable of 20 mph, it was not a commercial success, and it was not until 1903, with the model "A", that Ford cars took to the roads.

Fiat

The Fiat 3.5 hp of 1899 (2).

Renault

Views of the engine and interior of a 1906 Renault (3 and 4); a 1908 model (5); and one of the taxis pressed into service for the Battle of the Marne (12).

Benz

A replica of Benz's "Velocipede" (11); and three models dating from 1894, 1896 and 1898 (15).

Mercer

The legendary 35 Raceabouts of 1911 and 1912 (7 and 8).

Panhard

An 1895 model (14).

Citroën

A 1925 Citroën taxi (13); and a 1920 A-type (10).

Berliet

The 1907 60 hp model (9)

PREVIOUS PAGES: Nicolas Cugnot's artillery tractor (this was the second version, built in 1771); insets: a 1912 Panhard 20 hp, and a 1911 Mercer.

DELAGE • DELAHAYE DE DION BOUTON

Louis **Delage** was another of the brilliant engineers who added lustre to the motor car in the early years of the century. After training at the Ecole des Arts et Métiers, in Angers, he worked for Peugeot for many years before setting up his own company in 1905. Though short of capital, he had a wealth of bright ideas. Believing that an automobile should be fast and elegant, he evinced a life-long devotion to motor sport and to luxury travel. His sporting ambitions culminated in a victory at Indianapolis in 1914, a Grand Prix constructors' championship title in 1927, and some spectacular attempts on speed records in the early 1920s, when he fielded cars powered by one of the first ever V12 engines. He is also remembered for two prestigious models, the D6 and the D8; some major technical achievements, such as integral braking; and the shapely coupés he produced in the 1930s. Hard hit by the economic crisis, Louis Delage was forced to sell his company to Delahaye in 1935. Although he died in 1947, cars bearing his name continued to be produced until 1955.

Emile **Delahaye** gave little more than his name to a marque whose reputation suffered somewhat on account of the diversity of its interests: for many years the Delahaye company was known more for its military vehicles and specialised fire-engines than as a producer of quality cars. Delahaye is nonetheless one of the world's oldest makes, having begun production of automobiles in 1894. The company did not really make its mark, however, until Charles Weiffenbach took over in 1901, subsequently becoming one of the biggest pre-war concerns. The cars were amazingly robust and streamlined, like the famous 135 or the no-less-breathtaking 145 with its V12 engine. Unfortunately, its career was cut short by the war. Delahaye will also be remembered for some great racing achievements, such as Chaboud and Trémoulet's victory at Le Mans in 1938, won at an average speed of over 82 mph. In the early 1950s Delahaye was absorbed by the Hotchkiss company, and the name did not survive the takeover.

De Dion-Bouton was established in 1883 by Count Albert de Dion and his mechanic, Georges Bouton. The company first produced steam-powered vehicles, particularly tricycles, but in the period 1896 to 1933 – the year of its demise – it manufactured some famous models, such as the little "vis-à-vis" (so-called on account of its screw-type steering system) or the "Populaire". Although the company diversified its production in later years, these turn-of-the-century models remain the most attractive.

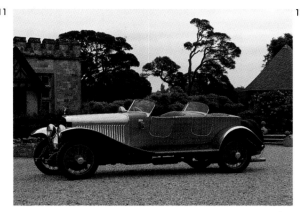

Delage

The four-cylinder, three-litre-engined Delage which won the Coupe de l'Auto in 1911 (12); two 1922 models (photos no.3 and 6); a 1924 model (13); a Dl S dating from 1924 (5); the 1933 Straight 8 (9); the famous D6, version 70, dating from 1937 (8); and some close-up shots: the radiator cap of a 1927 model (11), a steering wheel (14), and the coachwork of a 1924 machine (15).

Delahaye

Some fine examples of the Delahaye 135, whose launch coincided with the company's takeover of Delage in 1935 (1, 2 and 7); sports versions of this car scored victories at Le Mans in 1938 and in the French Grand Prix of 1949.

De Dion Bouton

A turn-of-the-century "vis-à-vis" model, produced in the years 1896 to 1900 (4); and the 16 hp model of 1904 (10).

ALFA-ROMEO • AMILCAR
AUBURN • BENTLEY • BMW
TALBOT-LAGO

Amilcar, a French marque founded in Paris in 1920, produced Asome of the most striking early sports cars. These included its very first model, the CC, which cruised at over 62 mph with considerable ease; its derivatives of the CGS range, which were eagerly sought after by the crowned heads of Europe; and the fabulous C6, only forty of which were ever built (1926 to 1939). This car broke countless speed records, exceeding 131 mph as early as 1926. The make did not survive the war.

Erret Cord will go down as the first great impresario of the still-young automobile industry. His commercial ability was akin to genius, enabling him to set up one company in his own name, manufacturing the prestigious Cord 810 and 812 models of the 1930s, and to inject life and vitality into two others: Duesenberg and **Auburn**. He bought the Auburn company from its founders in 1924, when, after twenty-five years in business it had run into serious financial trouble. The thoroughbred, often futuristic Auburn sports cars, such as the aluminium-bodied Cabin Speedster of 1929, were highly successful. Unfortunately, like many of their kind, they went out of production on the eve of the war, after which cars were never quite the same again.

We shall be turning the spotlight on **Alfa Romeo, Bentley**, and **BMW** in later chapters, but feel compelled to mention certain legendary models here in passing: the sumptuous, high-performance 3-litre saloons (and their descendants) created by William Owen Bentley in the 1920s and '30s; the first great sports car: the Alfa of the 1920s; and the BMW Dixi, a worthy successor to the Austin Seven, to which it owed so much. Talbot-Lago, as the old Talbot company was known after being taken over by Anthony Lago in 1934, built some of the finest French sports cars. Its high-quality creations ranged from Gran Turismo models – especially its superb cabriolets – to high-performance racers, one of which triumphed at Le Mans in 1950. Beset with insuperable financial difficulties, the company went out of business in 1956.

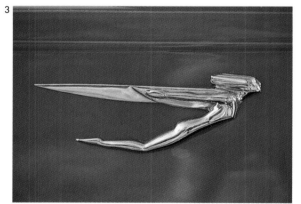

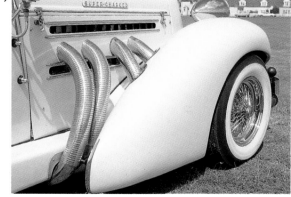

Amilcar
A 1926 version of the C6, which was powered by a six-cylinder engine with twin overhead camshafts (1).

Auburn
A selection of models from the Cord era: the Speedster and its winged mascot (3 and 8); the 1930 12-cylinder model (4); bodywork of a model dating from the mid-1930s (9); an 8/105 Phaeton, 1933 (15); an 8/51 dating from 1935 (12); and a collectors' replica (13 and 16).

Alfa-Romeo
The Alfa racing car, 1920 (2).

Bentley
A 1926 3-litre Bentley and close-up of its engine (6 and 7); and a 1929 4.5-litre model (10).

BMW
The original version of the Dixi, 1928 (5).

Talbot-Lago
A 1938 model (11); a 1948 Grand Sport (14); a 1950 4.5-litre racing model (17); and a 1955 2.5-litre coupé, the last model produced by the marque (18).

21

MARQUES OF DISTINCTION

ROLLS ROYCE

Charles Stuart Rolls was a man with a passion for competition. In 1900, while still at Cambridge, he was considered one of the United Kingdom's top racing drivers. As a young man of good background, he was accorded the great honour of introducing the Duke and Duchess of York – the future King George V and Queen Mary – to the joys of motoring. World record holder for the kilometre from a flying start, in 1903 he braved aristocratic prejudice by going into business and opening an agency for Panhard and Levassor in London. Familiar with the upper classes and convinced that there was a market for luxury cars, C.S. Rolls went into partnership with the celebrated engineer Frederick Henry Royce to produce a luxurious, quintessentially British motor car.

The first **Rolls-Royce** was unveiled at the 1904 London Motor Show. Very similar to F.H. Royce's Decauville, this model was distinguished by its classical radiator grill. The car was outstanding in the 1905 Tourist Trophy event, and immediately won a reputation for quality in Europe and the United States. Its international fame was consummated with the arrival of the Silver Ghost, of which 2,699 were built in the years 1908 to 1914.

C.S. Rolls, a keen aviator, was killed in a bi-plane in 1910. From the following year, all Rolls-Royces were sold with a radiator cap designed by the sculptor Charles Sykes. Formally known as the Spirit of Ecstasy, the emblem was commonly called the Flying Lady. It had been commissioned by Claude Johnson, who was outraged to see some Rolls-Royce owners adorn their radiator caps with "frivolous and grotesque mascots". Several versions were produced over the years, in one of which the "Lady" is kneeling. Contrary to legend, however, the emblem was always chromium or nickel-plated and never made of solid gold or silver. In the early years, just a few were gilded or silver-plated to order.

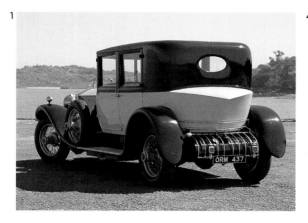

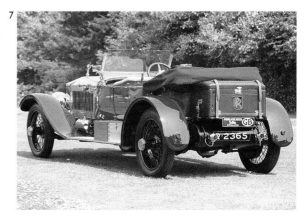

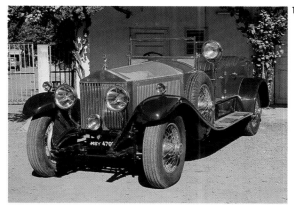

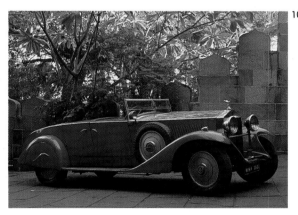

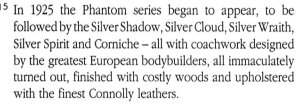

In 1925 the Phantom series began to appear, to be followed by the Silver Shadow, Silver Cloud, Silver Wraith, Silver Spirit and Corniche – all with coachwork designed by the greatest European bodybuilders, all immaculately turned out, finished with costly woods and upholstered with the finest Connolly leathers.

The tradition of comfort, silence and longevity has been maintained; Rolls-Royce, symbol of power and glory, synonymous with capitalism itself, is still considered the point of reference for any luxury limousine. In the assembly works at Crewe, where mass-production techniques are, of course, quite unknown, they still take time to produce "the best car in the world". For generations, a modest silence has surrounded the power output of its engine.

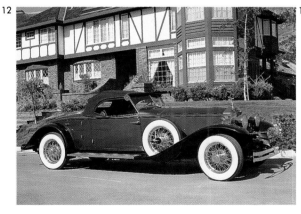

Examples of the Silver Ghost, dating from 1911 (4, 6 and 19); 1912 (5); and 1914 (3), with a close-up of the engine (15).
Silver Ghost Limousine, 1924 (1).
Phantom I, dating from 1925 (8); 1926 (13); and 1927 (2).
Alpine Eagle, 1913 (7).
20/25 models (9 and 10).
A 1923 Springfield (12); and Roadster (16).
Phantom III, 1938 (14).
Silver Wraith, 1946 (17).
Silver Cloud, 1961 (18).
Silver Wraith, 1979, close-up of Flying Lady (11).

Previous pages: Bugatti type 57 cabriolet Stelvio. Insets: 20 hp Rolls-Royce, 1927; and a 4-litre Alfa-Romeo 2900, 1938.

BENTLEY • LAGONDA AUSTIN PRINCESS

5

2

Bentley Motors Ltd, founded on 1 January 1919 by Walter Owen Bentley, should by rights have disappeared in the summer of 1931, when the company went into liquidation. In the event, it was bought by Rolls-Royce, whose management was attracted by the sporting image of the Bentley marque. (Its emblem, the winged B, had been designed by the automobile artist Gordon Crosby).

The first Bentley-Rolls produced at Derby had a V-shaped radiator grill and was baptized "the silent sports car" in reference to the marque's sporting past (five victories at Le Mans in the period 1924 to 1930). Though opulent, the Bentleys of the Rolls era have always maintained their sporting connotations, with a marked concern for streamlining. This was the case with the R series, ancestor of the Continental S1, a large, four-door limousine built at the Crewe works in 1958. It is also true of more recent versions: the S2 and S3, the T series, and other derivatives of the Rolls-Royce range, such as the fast Mulsanne Turbo, Turbo R (R for Roadholding) and Bentley Eight, which have firmer suspension than their Rolls-Royce cousins.

The Meadows-engined **Lagondas**, magnificent creations of the 1930s, together with certain Frazer-Nash and Aston-Martin machines, often go by the name of "post-vintage thoroughbreds". And some of the post-war models are equally delightful.

Lagonda was originally an American marque, founded in 1898 by Wilbur Gunn, a former opera singer who first tried his hand at motorcycle manufacturing. The marque went British after World War I, passing through several different hands. W.O. Bentley, who had left Rolls-Royce four years after the takeover of his own company, eventually came to the rescue. First engaged by the firm for the 1928 Le Mans event, he developed the 4.5-litre engine and designed a new V12. As technical adviser, he attempted, with A.

3

6

1

4

7

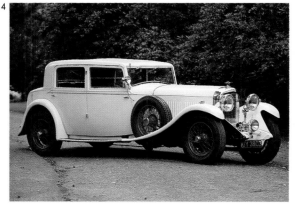

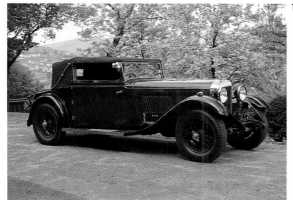

Good and R. Watney, to relaunch the marque in the years before World War II. Several luxury models date from this period, and victory at Le Mans in 1935 came just at the opportune moment. Unfortunately their efforts proved insufficient, and in 1947 Lagonda had again to be rescued, this time by David Brown. The marque was gradually absorbed by the Aston-Martin company, which retained the Lagonda name until the 1950s. The final Lagonda versions were powered by a 2.5 litre, six-cylinder engine.

Of the many British cars of distinction, it seems fitting to mention here the splendid **Austin Princess**, the most luxurious model produced by the Austin company.

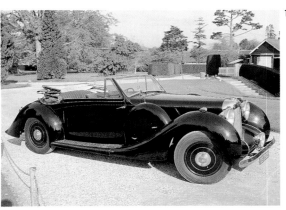

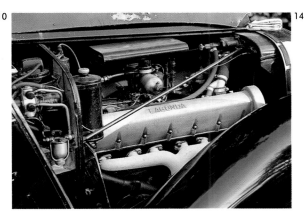

Bentley

Bentley "Classic car" (1).
Bentley Continental Type R, 1953 (2).
Bentley Mk6, 1951 (3).
Bentley 8 litre, 1930 (4).
Bentley 6.5 litre, 1928 (6).
Bentley Mulsanne Turbo (7).
1949 Bentley (8).
Bentley 4.5 litre, 1929 (9).
Bentley 8 litre Vanden Plas, 1931 (12).
Bentley 4.5 litre short-chassis version, 1928 (13).

Austin Princess

Austin Princess (5).

Lagonda

Lagonda 2.5, 1951 and its interior (11 and 17).
Lagonda V12, 1939 (10).
The V12 engine powering 1937 Lagonda models (14).
A Lagonda V12 of 1937 (15).
The radiador grille of the 2-litre Lagonda Continental of 1932 (16).

ALFA ROMEO • BMW SERIES 3 TRIUMPH ADLER JUNIOR

Established in 1910 and taken over six years later by Nicola Romeo, the Alfa company began producing sports cars in the 1920s. The RL Super Sport presented at the 1924 London Motor Show caused a sensation, but it was not until 1934, with Vittorio Jano contributing engineering genius, that **Alfa Romeo** really began to create cars of distinction. Designed for racing, the 6C-2300, together with the 68 hp Touring saloon and the 95 hp Pescara coupé, was the first in a line of magnificent performance machines: first the 200 hp 8C-2900 A Corsa Sport, a barchetta derived from the P3, then in 1936 a 4-litre, 12-cylinder machine developing 370 hp – Alfa's first 12-cylinder venture. These were followed in 1937 by the 8C 2900 B, then in 1939 by the new 6C 2500 range in more comfortable saloon, sports and spider SS Corsa versions, with power outputs of between 87 and 125 hp. At the time, the magnificent 6C 2500 SS cost the equivalent of two Rolls-Royces!

The firm set up by Karl Rapp and Max Friz in 1916, which became **BMW** (Bayerische Motoren Werk) two years later, first made its name designing marine and aircraft engines and manufacturing motorcycles. Not until 1933 did it produce its first motor car: the 303, which was powered by a straight-six engine. The 303 was followed by the 1.5-litre 315 and the 1.9-litre 319, then, in 1937, by the 326. A subtle mix of elegance and aggression, its ultra-low, streamlined appearance was something quite new. Designed with the help of a wind tunnel, its drag coefficient was astonishingly low: a cd value of only 0.32! It was the first BMW fitted with the "double-bean" radiator grill. Its sporting derivative, the 327, was available in cabriolet and coupé versions. Strangely, these two models stem from the 328, the thousandth exemplar of which had come off the production line a year before. The 328 was in production from 1936 to 1940; the 326 and 327 from late 1936 to 1941. It is outrageous that the 326 was copied in East Germany under the name EMW until the mid-1950s, by when 500 of the cars had been produced. They are distinguishable by their less refined bumpers and other clumsy readjustments. The first post-war BMW, the 501 saloon, inaugurated a quite different style.

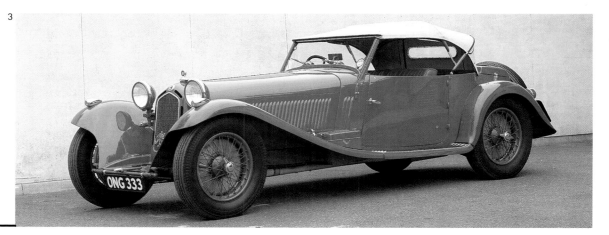

In England, on the eve of the war, the **Triumph** company was labouring under serious financial constraints, despite having produced some attractive models. In the early 1930s, the Gloria sold well, though of its successor, the Dolomite, only three examples were ever built. It was in fact an almost exact copy by Donald Healey of the 2.3-litre Alfa Romeo! The last genuine pre-war Triumph was the Adler Junior, introduced in 1939, the year in which the firm went bankrupt. Triumph was bought out by Sheffield Steel, shortly before war was declared.

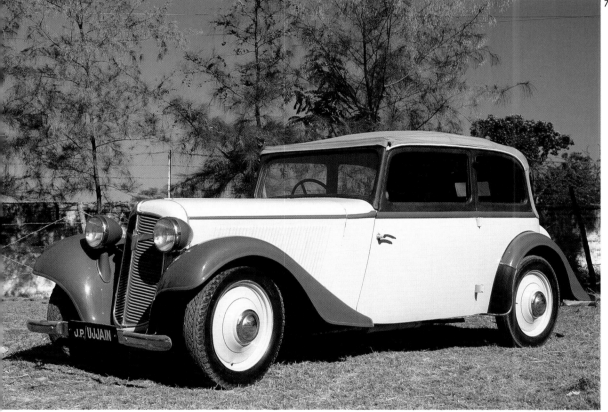

Alfa Romeo

On the eve of the war, Alfa Romeo was producing various versions of the 8C 2900 (1, 2 and 4).
Born to race: the Alfa Romeo 8C 2300, engineered by Vittorio Jano, first appeared in 1934 (3).
The Alfa Romeo RL, unveiled at the London Motor Show in 1924 (5).

Triumph

The 1939 Triumph Adler Junior (7).

BMW

BMW's third model was introduced in 1935 (6); The BMW 328: a streamlined machine, introduced in 1936 (8 and 9); A BMW drophead (10).

DE TOMASO • FACEL-VEGA

Introduced in 1970, the **De Tomaso** Pantera is the most enduring of modern GT cars. Seven thousand have been produced to date, in a number of different versions.

It was back in 1959 that Alessandro de Tomaso, an Argentinian by birth, decided to build "a civilised Ford GT 40". He set himself up in the Ferrari stronghold of Modena and began to work on a coupé with a Ford 1500 engine, entrusting the design work to Ghia. The result, unveiled in 1965, was the Vallelunga, of which only a few were produced. De Tomaso's second project was more ambitious. He called in Ghia and Vignale to help him design another GT car with a centrally mounted engine, in this case powered by a big Ford V8, 4.7-litre engine. The Mangusta was introduced in 1968.

De Tomaso was then set for a major operation. His original plan was to build 5,000 cars a year for export to the United States. Designed by the Ghia stylist Tom Tjaarda, the Pantera came on stream in 1970. It was a sophisticated sports car, aggressive and low-slung (3ft 6 in/1.10m), powered by the extremely rugged Ford Cleveland "351" V8, a 5.7-litre, cast-iron engine. Although De Tomaso also brought out the Deauville (1970) and Longchamp (1972) models, the Pantera remained the firm favourite. The most recent version was introduced a few years ago.

Since buying out Maserati, Alessandro de Tomaso has abandoned his own marque, and only a trickle of the cars are now being produced.

Jean-Clément Daninos – brother of the creator of Major Thompson – worked as a metallurgical engineer with Citroën on their Traction model and with the aircraft constructor Morane-Saulnier. But he nourished a private dream: to build a car of his own. A customer of Bentley, he wanted to produce a car as sophisticated as England's best.

In 1939, he founded Facel (Forges et Ateliers de Construction d'Eure-et-Loir). The company produced the aluminium bodywork for the first Dyna Panhard, then for the Simca 8 and 9 models and the Ford-Comète. He was employing a workforce of 1,700 by 1948, when he brought out the Cresta, a de-luxe, streamlined automobile with a Bentley engine and chassis. Seventeen of the cars were produced.

Three years later he designed a prototype and signed an agreement with Chrysler, who were to supply an engine. Work began in 1952, and the first **Facel-Vega** emerged in

6

7

10

8

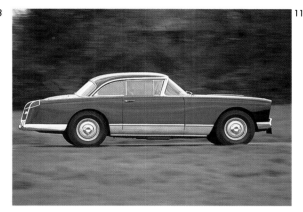

11

12

9 1954, winning universal approval at the Paris Motor Show. A superb car, it sold for FFr2.8 million – the equivalent of six Renault 4 CVs. The eleven original 4.5-litre FVs were followed by a further 330, as successive versions of the car were developed between 1955 and 1958. The year 1958 saw the arrival of the HK 500, the fastest four-seater coupé of its time (148 mph), which was produced alongside the Facel II HK2 in the years 1958 to 1964. The Facel II was the last model powered by the Chrysler engine, others being fitted with a 4-cylinder Pont-à-Mousson.

Lacking the support of a major car manufacturer, France's last prestige marque went out of business in the mid 1960s.

De Tomaso

More than 7,000 Panteras have been manufactured since 1970. These pictures show the GTS model (1, 2, 4 and 7). The De Tomaso Deauville (3 and 5). The De Tomaso prototype (6).

Facel-Vega

The remarkable Facel-Vega HK 500, which hads a top speed of 148 mph (8, 11 and 12). The Facel-Vega Facelia (10) and the Facel Vega II of 1962 (9).

BUGATTI

Bugatti's total output, in just over twenty years, was in the region of 7,500 cars: 2,000 less than Ford or Chevrolet were producing in a single day on the eve of the Great Depression in 1929.

Bugatti might well have been an Italian marque, had not Ettore Bugatti emigrated from his native land; or German, if Alsace, where he had chosen to settle, had remained under German rule at the end of World War I. Though of Milanese parentage, Ettore was a Frenchman at heart. His father, Carlo, had been a friend of Tolstoy and Puccini. A lute-maker and architect, he was one of the most renowned cabinet-makers of his day. As early as 1910, when he set up his factory at Molsheim, Ettore Bugatti's declared aim was to build a car superior in quality even to a Hispano-Suiza or a Rolls-Royce. For the time being he lacked the financial resources, but he was already applying a principle from which he never departed: there must be no suggestion of compromise in the building of a Bugatti. His criteria were speed and beauty, regardless of production expenses, sale price or running costs.

Ettore Bugatti had an innate sense of functionality and remained faithful to his vision. A strong personality, he hated routine and often stuck to outdated methods, generally aiming at simplicity, but sometimes introducing complications as he saw fit. Whether we consider his spartan thoroughbred racing cars or the superlatively safe, fast, powerful and silent Royales – "the royal car never owned by a King" – Bugatti will always be one of the great motoring legends, and the purest expression of art as applied to the design of an automobile.

After competing in the first motor races and collaborating with Prinetti and Stucchi, de Dietrich, Mathis and Deutz, in 1910 "the wizard" set to work on a car bearing his own name: the Bugatti Type 13, the first model with the distinctive horseshoe-shaped radiator. It was a small car

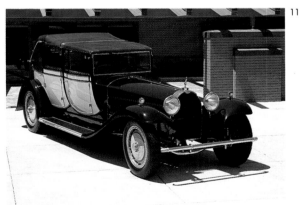

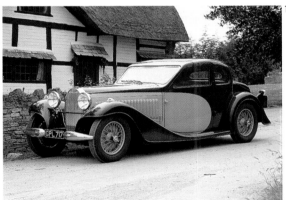

with a 1300cc engine, and a breath-taking top speed of 59 mph! It met with instant success. In 1911, Bugatti's workforce increased to 65, and in that year 75 cars were produced. Encouraged by his success on the race track, Ettore Bugatti then dreamed of a more comfortable motor car. The Type 15 was the ancestor of his high-performance saloons. It was followed by the BB, built under licence to Peugeot, then a big 5-litre motor capable of 103 mph. On the eve of World War I, the Molsheim factory was employing 200 workers. When it was requisitioned by the Germans, Ettore Bugatti fled to Italy. He took two cars with him, having first buried the new engines he was working on. From Milan, he made his way back to Paris, where he served as an air force engineer and designed two aircraft engines. One of these – a 24.3-litre monster – was later the starting point for his kingly Royale, and also served to drive a railcar. Returning to Molsheim after the Armistice, Bugatti set to work to rebuild his business.

The Type 44, which appeared in 1927, was powered by a remarkably flexible 3-litre engine (1).
The distinctive logo: part of the Bugatti legend (2).
A Bugatti racing car: the 37 A of 1927 (3 and 15).
The Type 37 was a development of the Brescia (4).
The Bugatti Open 2-Seat Blue (5).
Ettore Bugatti (1881-1947) came to Molsheim in 1902 (6).
The Bugatti Type 43 (7).
The celebrated 35, which was introduced in 1924 (8).
The Bugatti Type MA, 1933 (9).
Jean Bugatti was responsible for the styling of the 57 (10).
Two examples of the superlative Bugatti Royale saloons (11 and 12).
A Type 57 Ventoux of 1937 (13).
The Bugatti 55 (14).
Approximately 750 Type 57s were manufactured in the years 1934 to 1938 (16).

BUGATTI

By 1920, **Bugatti** was back, reaping success upon success: 10,000 racing victories and 37 world records! The cars were engaged on all fronts: first the "tank" models, then the unbeatable Type 35, with 1000 wins to its credit, and the 51, which took up the running in 1931. The following year, a four-wheel drive vehicle, the Type 53, was tested on the race track, and the 54 Grand Prix version beat the world record at over 133 mph on the Avus circuit in Berlin. in 1937, the 57 G (top speed 140 mph, with average fuel consumption of 20 litres per 100km) was the winner at Le Mans. But the greatest achievement belongs to the 50 B, which broke the 200 mph barrier (206.25 mph) during the Coupe des Prisonniers held at the Bois de Boulogne in September 1945.

It is difficult to distinguish sports cars from racing versions. It is also no easy task to trace the development of Bugatti's fast, comfortable GT cars. Before 1914, types 13, 15 and 17 had appeared and, shortly before the outbreak of war, types 22 and 23. Pursuing his dream of building "a car bigger than a Rolls-Royce but considerably lighter", at the 1921 Paris Motor Show Ettore Bugatti exhibited his Type 28, powered by a V8 engine in aluminium. The following year he brought out the Type 30, and in 1926 the 38 and 40 models. But Bugatti was still not satisfied and, with his son Jean, continued to work on his masterpiece: the Royale or "Golden Bugatti". The prototype was built in 1926. It had a 4.57-metre wheelbase, a 6-metre chassis, and a 14.7-litre 8-cylinder engine. Though never measured, the power output has been estimated at 300 hp, giving the three-ton monster a top speed of 125 mph! Bugatti was thinking in terms of 25 cars. In the end, only seven chassis and eleven bodies were built between 1926 and 1935. The first completed car was not sold until 1932, to a German gynaecologist. The third and last order was placed by a British industrialist. A Royale cost three times more than the most expensive Rolls-Royce. The coupé version unveiled at the 1928 Paris Motor Show was priced at FFr

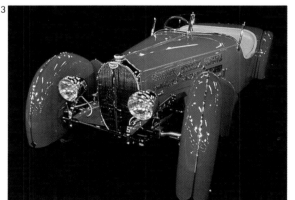

697,000; at the time, a primary school teacher was earning less than FFr 1,000 a month.

Ettore Bugatti handed over the business to his son Jean in 1936, but Jean was killed in a road accident three years later. His monument, the Type 64, came into production on the eve of World War II. It was to be the last true Bugatti. Ettore Bugatti's second son, Roland, in conjunction with Pierre Marco, presented the 101, a derivative of the 57, at the 1951 Paris Motor Show, but it lacked the distinctive Bugatti personality. The era of Bugatti and his Molsheim thoroughbreds was over.

An emblem associated with both luxury and racing (1)
The Type 57 Atlantic (2, 5 and 7).
A Bugatti in the Blackhawk collection (3).
The third body for the Royale (Type 41) dating from 1927 (4 and 11).
Gandini's design for the EB 110 (6).
Bugatti Type 59 (8).
A 1932 Type 55 Roadster (9).
A 1934 Bugatti Type 46 (10).
A 1936 version of the "Tank", (12)
A Type 57 S of 1936 vintage (13).
First outing of the "mulet" No.0 (prototype 2) at the factory (14).

HISPANO-SUIZA • AUDI • BMW ALPINE-RENAULT • PANHARD

In the late 1930s and in the post-war years, several cars stood out on account of their bold design or revolutionary features.

Founded in 1904 by Damian Mateu I. Bisa and a group of Swiss industrialists, **Hispano-Suiza** could claim to be a truly European marque: though based in Barcelona, some of its cars were produced at the Bois-Colombes factory, in France. Its cars were highly prized by the Spanish royal family, and models bearing the stork emblem were sought after for both racing and driving about town. This was especially true of the majestic V-12s, with coachwork by such great names as Kellner and Vanvooren. After the interruption of the war years, the firm concentrated on building aircraft.

The **Audi** company first made a name for itself with its magnificent 225, introduced onto the market in 1936.

In Germany again, the **BMW** 315/1 Touring Sport (40 hp/75 mph) was the first in a line of increasingly powerful cars, heralding the fluid lines of the 327 and especially the 328. The 501 and 503 models of the post-war years marked a break with the pre-war series 3, but the great innovation was the splendid 507 roadster with V8 aluminium engine, which made its appearance in the late 1950s. This BMW was a worthy reply to the redoubtable Mercedes 300 and 300 SL, but unfortunately was not a commercial success.

France has never lacked its share of prestigious motor cars. Heir to a long tradition of luxury 6- and 8-cylinder saloons and limousines, the **Panhard** Dynamic was the first de-luxe car with monocoque chassis. What is amazing about this big, streamlined saloon is its driving position, with room for passengers on either side of the driver!

In the 1960s the motoring revolution owed much to Jean Rédélé, who built a sports car body to clothe the motorised chassis of the 4 CV **Renault**. After the A.106 and the A.108 came the A.110 1100 sporting saloon, subsequently augmented to 1300, 1440 and 1500cc and culminating, in 1967, in the famous 1600. The S and 1800 versions derived from it figured prominently in motor sport from 1969 to 1978, and enabled Renault to win the world rallying championship in 1973.

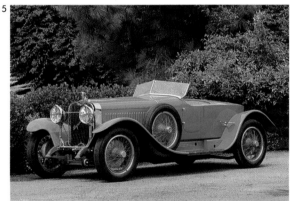

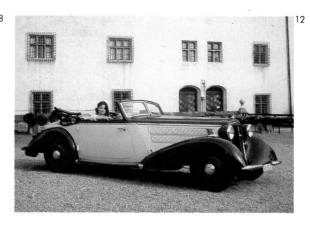

Hispano-Suiza

Some remarkable achievements by the firm of Hispano-Suiza: the V12 convertible Type 68b of 1934 (1); one of the early models, dating from 1919 (4); the Hispano 45 model 9 of 1928 (5); two Hispano-Suiza models (2 and 6); the 1933 V 12 (9); and the Tulip Wood of 1924 (11).

Panhard

The original Panhard Dynamic of 1937 (3).

BMW

The pre-war 315/1 (13); and the post-war 503 cabriolet (1957) and 507 models (10 and 7).

Alpine-Renault

The famous Alpine-Renault A.110, 1600 S sports saloon (8).

Audi

The 1937 Audi 225 (12).

AMERICAN
OPULENCE

DUESENBERG • PACKARD HUDSON • BUICK

Duesenberg will always remain the apotheosis of the luxury American automobile. The car one pictures in one's mind's eye is being driven over the hills of Hollywood by Clark Gable or Gary Cooper, who were among the happy few Duesenberg owners. The Indianapolis company, founded by the Duesenberg brothers in 1904, only began producing cars seriously in 1918, was taken over by Errett Cord in 1928, and went out of business nine years later. In that time, production volumes were never high. Models included the "A" (500 manufactured between 1918 and 1926), a racing version of which won the Indianapolis 500 three times and the 1921 French Grand Prix – the only American victory of its kind; the "X" (just 12 cars!); and the fabulous "J" (known as the "SJ" after 1932), which, together with certain Bugatti and Rolls Royce models, must represent the highest achievement in automobile engineering.

Furious at having a brand new motor car break down on him, in 1899 James **Packard** founded one of the most prestigious of American marques, symbolizing, with Pierce-Arrow and Peerless – also now defunct – the splendours of a bygone era. When the company went out of business in 1957, Packard had produced only a little over one-and-a-half-million automobiles, but all were of the highest standard, especially the famous Twin Six, dating from 1915, whose V12 engine was the wonder of its day.

Hudson cars were a prime example of what today we would call the bottom end of the luxury car market. Founded in 1908 and named after the man who put up the capital, the marque always set out to give those who could not afford a luxury limousine at least the illusion of owning a car of distinction. The company produced vast numbers of cars, until it closed down in 1954. Some of its outstanding achievements were the extremely comfortable Super Six series (1916) and the so-called "Step Down" models of the late 1940s.

Buick is synonymous with the solid and luxurious American car – but at a reasonable price, rather like Chrysler or Dodge. Founded in 1903 by David Buick, a mechanic of Scottish ancestry, the company was the driving force behind the establishment, in 1908, of General Motors. Thanks to its 1930s limousines with their durable 8-cylinder engines and the big coupé versions of the 1950s, Buick has remained a household name, even though modern Buicks lack something of their former prestige.

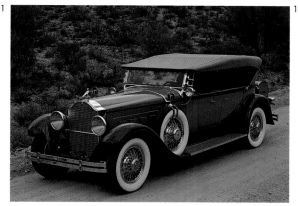

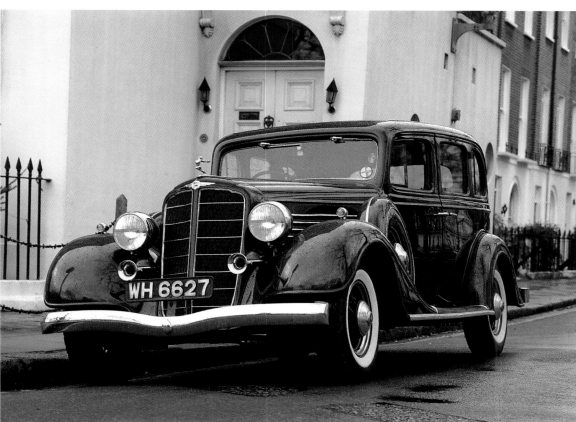

Duesenberg

Three models from the famous J Series (1, 2 and 5); they were powered by a 6.8-litre straight-eight engine, generating over 250 hp.

Packard

The Twin Six (11); and a custom 645 Dietrich (14).

Hudson

The Big Six, dating from 1925 (4); a 1934 Terraplane (3); and a Commodore Eight Convertible of 1950 (6).

Buick

Two sedan models: a 1935 series 50 (9) and a two-door Special with V8 engine from the 1960s (8); two Riviera Silver models from the late 1970s (7 and 10).

Dodge and Chrysler

A 1959 Dodge Custom Royal (12) and 1934 Convertible version (15); a 1949 Chrysler Town and Country (13).

Previous pages: a 1953 Buick Skylark Convertible; insets, left to right: a 1937 Buick Century, and a Duesenberg J cabriolet as redesigned by Graber.

CADILLAC

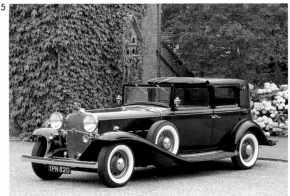

Marquis Antoine de la Mothe **Cadillac**, the Gascon nobleman who, in 1710, founded the town of d'Etroit in the name of the King of France, would have been amazed to know that this small settlement on the shores of lake Erie was one day to become a world centre of automobile engineering, and that his own name was to grace a distinguished make of car. Yet, for almost a hundred years, no name has better symbolized the power and glory of the American car industry than Cadillac. Whether in terms of beauty, robustness, performance or technical innovation, the cars of this marque – integrated since 1909 into the giant General Motors company – are among the most successful and celebrated America has produced.

The firm was born on 22 August 1902, in Detroit, from the ashes of the company previously established by William Murphy and Henry Ford – the latter having left to set up on his own. The new boss was Henry Leland, whose motto was: "Our creed is perfection; our rule precision". Leland created the small Model A Cadillac, which first appeared in 1903, developing it over twenty years through versions all the way down to "T". Cadillac will also be remembered for some important technical innovations: standardisation of manufacture (in 1908, for instance, three Cadillacs were stripped down, the parts scrambled and all three cars reassembled, each performing flawlessly); in 1912, the electric starter (invented by Charles Kettering); in 1928, the synchronised gearbox; and, in 1954, power-assisted steering.

When Lawrence Fisher took over as director of the company in 1925, Cadillac became the very first marque to set up a styling department, managed by the brilliant Harley Earl, who set his inimitable seal on new models. The rounded bodywork of the 1930s, tail fins of aeronautical inspiration in the 1940s, the elongated lines of the 1950s … in every period, Cadillac was distinguished by a style of its own, often revolutionary, always majestic. In recent years, overconcerned to counter the inroads of German luxury cars, Cadillac has unfortunately been too ready to standardize the bodywork of its models.

7

12

17

8

13

18

9

14 The very first Cadillac of 1903 (4) was powered by a 1.6-litre single-cylinder engine.

The 1930s: Cadillac's masterpiece, the 452, with the fabulous V16 engine (1, 2 and 5); two examples of the 75: the 7 Passenger, and a series with bodywork by Fleetwood (8 and 3); close-up of the radiator mascot (9). The post-war period: the 1947 Special Body (6); the 1954 Model 75 limousine (10); three versions of the famed Eldorado: a 1957 Brougham (12), a 1957 Biarritz with close-up of the driving position (13 and 18), and a convertible (17).

The 1960s: the superb lines of the 1963 Coupé De Ville (7 and 11); two examples of the 1969 Eldorado Fleetwood (14 and 15).

Today: a 1990 Eldorado (16).

10

15

11

16

LINCOLN • DE SOTO • FORD

The **Lincoln** company was set up in 1918 by Henry Leland, former head and founder of Cadillac. At the age of seventy-four, having quit General Motors, he thought it would be a challenge to build aero-engines! But falling demand at the end of the war turned his attention back to automobile manufacture, so the marque was born almost by chance. He named it after Abraham Lincoln, a man he enormously admired. Wanting to create a luxury car on Cadillac lines, in 1920 he brought out the prototype of a Torpedo model, with a V8 engine closely modelled on those he had manufactured at Detroit. In 1922, having encountered serious financial difficulties, Leland put Lincoln up for sale. Henry Ford was the buyer, partly because his group needed a top-of-the-range line, partly to enable his son Edsel to launch his business career. Edsel Ford quickly revolutionized the company, making Lincoln one of America's most prestigious marques. In particular, he set out to create spacious, luxury cars with aesthetic appeal. With the arrival of the Zephyr, in 1933, and the Continental, in 1939, the marque reached the height of its fame. Since then, the Continental range has been constantly updated (Mark II, Mark III, etc.), losing nothing of its lustre over the decades.

In 1928, wanting to increase its share of the market, the Chrysler company decided to create a middle-of-the-range marque. The result was **De Soto**, whose cars were long known as "the Indestructibles" on account of their unparalleled toughness. Before the war the cars sold well, mainly because they were competitively priced (less then $400 for the CK model, which came out in 1930). When production began again in 1946, the emphasis was on more sophisticated and luxurious models. Though well made, they never enjoyed commercial success, and the marque was wound up at the close of the 1950s.

We have discussed the Model T **Ford** in an earlier chapter and shall be examining the marque in more detail later. But while on the subject of opulent American cars, we feel bound to mention two or three Ford models. There was the Thunderbird of the 1950s, for instance, or the legendary Mustang, which was introduced in 1963 and achieved overnight success. Its annual sales figures continued at over half a million throughout the 1960s. The Mustang was the creation of Ford's wonder boy, Lee Iacocca, and did much to renew the image of American cars, Ford in particular. The same can be said of models designed by foreign subsidiaries of the company, two examples of which are shown here.

Lincoln

Two examples of the Zephyr, designed in 1933 by Bob Gregory; one dates from 1935, the other from 1937 (7 and 11). The Continental, standard bearer of the marque over many years: a 1958 Mk III (2), a 1984 Mk VII (3), two classic models (8 and 10), and a recent majestic, six-door version (6).

De Soto

A 1951 Custom (5); a 1959 Adventurer (12); and a 1960 version of the Adventurer (9), the last model produced by the company, powered by a 300 hp engine. Though a fine car, it did not prevent De Soto from going under.

Ford

Three examples of the Mustang, the first two dating from 1965 and 1966, the third from 1984 (13, 14 and 15). Two foreign-built Fords: the British Zephyr and Zodiac, dating from the early 1960s (1 and 4). With the Mustang, they helped renew Ford's image.

CHEVROLET • CHRYSLER • DODGE
PONTIAC • OLDSMOBILE

Chevrolet is something of a misnomer. In fact, Louis Chevrolet, a brilliant racing driver in the early days, who was born in Switzerland and had emigrated to America in 1900, left the company almost as soon as it was founded. The year was 1913, and his co-founder, William Durant, rich Michigan financier and head of the powerful General Motors group, quickly discouraged his associate by constant financial manoeuvring. Poor Louis eventually came "home" – ruined – in 1933, to work as a simple mechanic at the Detroit factory! It is also a fact that, unlike Ford, Chevrolet, which has undoubtedly sold more cars than any other make this century, has never really produced a legendary car. Even the Corvette, its most celebrated sports car, though it has gone through innumerable versions, has never really attained to all-time greatness. Even so, in eighty years of manufacturing, Chevrolet has produced some fine models of all kinds, from the utilitarian to the sporty, from the most ordinary to the most extravagant.

The history of **Chrysler**, the third biggest American automobile group after General Motors and Ford, begins with a fabulous success story: its founder, Walter Percy Chrysler, started life as a Kansas farmer's son. He became in turn mechanic, engineer, director of Buick in 1912, then second-in-command at General Motors, before launching out on his own. The marque has been very prolific, especially after it began to set up foreign subsidiaries. Rather like Chevrolet, Chrysler has always lacked an obvious flagship. Unfortunately, the fabulous Airflow, launched in 1934, whose aerodynamic lines and revolutionary design maybe came before their time, was not a commercial success. The Town and Country, introduced after the war (see pp.40-41), is a better symbol of Chrysler's obsession with creating spacious, utilitarian cars. This policy the company has always followed.

Dodge, set up at the beginning of the century by two brothers, John and Horace Dodge, was eventually absorbed by the Chrysler group in 1928. Obviously robust and, like **Oldsmobile** and **Pontiac** models, always classical in inspiration, Dodge cars embody one aspect of the enduring legend of the American automobile. Faced with Japanese – and to a lesser extent European – competition, the industry is currently finding it difficult to maintain its poise.

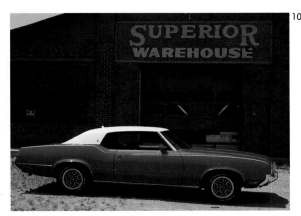

Chevrolet

Two examples of the Corvette: a 1963 Stingray and a 1968 Stingray L88 (4 and 11).

Chrysler

A 1956 New Yorker (2), and the 1980 version of the same car (5); a 1987 Le Baron turbo, with close-up of the driving position (3 and 6).

Dodge

A "500" model from the 1970s (12); two shots of the fast 1969 Daytona (7 and 8).

Oldsmobile

A 1972 Cutlass Supreme (10).

Pontiac

A selection of sports models: the 1979 Firebird TransAm (1); the 1979 GrandAm sport coupé (13); the 1987 Sunbird (9); and the 1988-1990 Grand Prix (14 and 15).

ITALIAN STYLE

FERRARI

In 1945, when Enzo **Ferrari** established his manufacturing firm, he was forty-seven years old. He already had a quarter century of achievements to his credit, first as a racing driver, then as organizer of his own racing team. In an Italy still reeling from the effects of the war, he risked his all: in November 1946 he announced his intention to give up making machine tools and concentrate on sports and racing cars. Only three cars were produced in 1947, the first to bear the famous prancing horse emblem. It had formerly graced the cockpit of World War I fighter ace Francesco Baracca, who eventually met his death on Mount Montello. Countess Paolina Baracca had predicted that the black horse on a yellow ground (the colour of Modena) would bring Ferrari luck.

The Ferrari factory at Maranello then began to produce a steady but limited stream of fast racing machines and hand-crafted sports models. In the words of Enzo Ferrari: "I have never been a major constructor, nor have aspired to become one. I remain a provincial craftsman". In fact, Ferrari has never produced more than 4,000 cars a year, not wishing to jeopardize the marque's exclusivity. According to the famous advertising slogan: "A Ferrari is not something you can buy; it's something you long for ...". Though now under the control of Fiat, Ferrari has never departed from this principle. For the Ingegniere's successors, the continuing challenge will be to marry craftsmanship with advanced technology.

At auction, Ferraris are undoubtedly the most beautiful, expensive, sought after and inaccessible of all cars. Acceptance of one's order for a thoroughbred of this kind is a sign of the highest personal success. On the race track, despite the marque's present discomfiture in Formula 1, the prancing horse remains the symbol of top-level competition. So it has been since 25 May 1947, when Cortese, driving a Type 125 on the Rome circuit, scored Ferrari's first race victory.

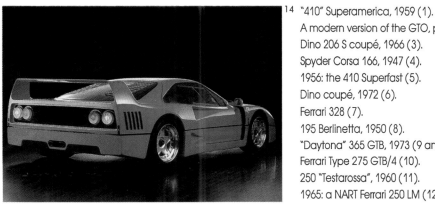

"410" Superamerica, 1959 (1).

A modern version of the GTO, produced in 1985 (2).

Dino 206 S coupé, 1966 (3).

Spyder Corsa 166, 1947 (4).

1956: the 410 Superfast (5).

Dino coupé, 1972 (6).

Ferrari 328 (7).

195 Berlinetta, 1950 (8).

"Daytona" 365 GTB, 1973 (9 and 13).

Ferrari Type 275 GTB/4 (10).

250 "Testarossa", 1960 (11).

1965: a NART Ferrari 250 LM (12).

Ferrari F.40, 1988 (14).

The Testarossa (15)

The 4-litre GTO, 1962 (16).

Engine compartment of the 365 GTC, 1967 (17).

Spyder Dino 246 GT, 1974 (18).

PREVIOUS PAGES: Ferrari F 40, 1988. Insets, left to right: Lamborghini Countach LP 500 S, 1984, and Maserati Merak.

ISOTTA-FRASCHINI LAMBORGHINI

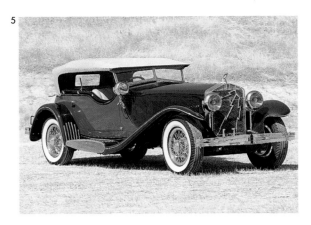

The Italians Cesare Isotta and Vincenzo Fraschini began importing Renaults in 1899. These provided the inspiration for their own cars, powered by large-capacity Mercedes engines, first produced in 1903. By the time the Tipo C.A. (capacity 11.3 litres!) came out four years later, **Isotta-Fraschini** ranked second only to Fiat, and the firm's success continued into the post-war years. During the 1920s, Isotta-Fraschini models, fitted with powerful 8-cylinder engines, became even more luxurious. Prestigious automobiles, they provided a standard of reference until the late 1930s.

Ferruccio **Lamborghini**, who had set up an agricultural tractor business in 1949, turned his hand to building sports cars out of sheer enthusiasm. In 1961, by when he was Italy's third biggest manufacturer of agricultural machinery, he set out to produce "the most perfect GT car in the world". He bought a 90,000-square-metre site near Modena and hired some skilled Ferrari craftsmen, including Carlo Chiti and Bizzarini, the creator of the renowned GTO. In 1963, after experiments with a prototype, he was ready to implement his project for the first "anti-Ferrari" bearing his bull emblem. Thirteen of the 350 GTs were produced in 1964, and by 1967 the run had reached 141. From this car were derived the 400 GT 2+2, again designed by Bertone, and the fabulous Miura, a direct rival to the Ferrari Daytona. When it came out in 1964, it incorporated all the experience acquired on the race track by the Sant'Agata engineers: Dallara, Stanzani and Wallace.

Designed by the young Bertone stylist Marcello Gandini (who was also responsible for the Stratos), the car was powerful and of impeccable pedigree. Its 440 hp V12 engine gave it a top speed of 187 mph. In all, 779 of the cars were produced, in several different versions. But neither the Miura, the Marzal, the Espada (1968), the Countach (1971) nor the Urraco (1972) was ever entered for a race: Ferruccio Lamborghini would not have it.

In 1972, following cancellation of a big tractor order by the Bolivian government, Lamborghini sold a 51 per cent stake to a Swiss businessman, G.H. Rossetti, and gradually lost interest in the business. Severely shaken by the oil crisis, then left in the lurch by BMW for the production of the M1, Lamborghini struggled on until the early 1980s, when a French industrialist took the company in hand. After the Jalpa, the Countach LP 5000 and the "all-terrain" LM, the firm's catalogue now lists only one model: the Diablo.

ITALIAN STYLE

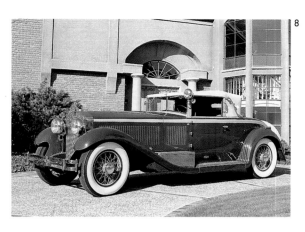

Isotta-Fraschini

A distinguished pre-war marque, Isotta-Fraschini produced some magnificent big-engined cars. Illustrated here are a 1928 coupé (8); a Castagna-designed phaeton 8 ASS dating from 1930 (1); and a 1933 Tipo 8 ASS (5), with a view of the sophisticated, typically Italian driving position (6).

Lamborghini

The futuristic Countach first appeared in 1971 and has run through a number of versions (2, 7, 11, 12, 13 and 15), the most recent being the 5000 S "Quattrovalvole", unveiled in 1985 (4). The Miura spyder (3 and 14).
Rival to the Ferrari 365 GTB 4 Daytona, for many purists the Miura is "the most beautiful car ever built" (9).
The 1969 Miura: 440 hp and a top speed of 187 mph (10).

MASERATI

Founded in 1914 by the four **Maserati** brothers, the Trident marque has had something of a chequered history. Deeply involved in motor racing after 1926, Maserati eventually came under the control of Adolfo Orsi, who in 1937 bought out all the family members and attempted to broaden the company's activities. Not long after, he unveiled the marque's first sporting saloon, the A6G 1500, which was followed by the 2000 and the A6-GCS.

Even so, Maseratis were bought only by a very restricted public. Not until the 1950s were GT versions introduced, in particular the 3500 GT, a jewel of a car, albeit slightly kitsch. Designed to appeal to the stars of popular entertainment, the 240 hp, 6-cylinder model was a success. Maserati sold 2,000 of them in the years 1957 to 1965, offering an alternative to Ferrari at a considerably lower price.

Its successor was the Mistral, regarded as the most successful sports car of its day. But, despite its growing fame, the Italian marque was unable to balance its books. In 1968, Adolfo Orsi was forced to call it a day. Citroën took over the business – and a mountain of debts. Such were the losses that, in 1975, the French constructor in turn threw in the towel.

With the support of a few partners and a subsidy from the Italian government, Alessandro De Tomaso then took up the challenge. To restore the business, he dusted down plans for a 2+2 coupé originally designed by Ghia. The styling was revised by Frua and the engine compartment adapted to receive the Maserati V8, which had previously powered its Indy, Ghibli, Khamsin and Bora models. The result was the Kyalami. Subsequent efforts were concentrated on producing the Bi-turbo, which gave the marque a much-needed boost. Less aggressive in style, the present range includes the 222, the 430, a 2.8-litre spyder version, and the Shamal.

A 1949 Maserati coupé (1).

The classic Ghibli in both roadster and Coupé form (2).

The Maserati Bora (3 and 6).

An 8 CM racing car, dating from 1934 (4).

The Mistral 3700 (5).

A 2000 saloon version (7).

A new-look Maserati: the Bi-turbo (8).

A Khamsin of 1980 vintage (9).

A 6-cylinder Maserati (10).

The aggressively styled Ghibli (11).

A 1980 Merak SS (12).

The Maserati Kyalami (13).

The Maserati Karif (14).

The 9000 GT version (15).

SOME
CURIOSITIES

THE BODY-BUILDERS

In the first half of the century, it was usual to make a distinction between the mechanical part of an automobile and its coachwork. This reflected current construction methods and the volume of cars being produced. The vulgarization of the motor car and its almost systematic industrialization in the early 1950s revolutionized methods, with the result that the ubiquitous craftsman of yesteryear has been replaced by styling departments, one for each major constructor.

Only a few independent body-builders remain, the great names, most of them Italian, who are engaged by the big manufacturers to design prestige models or by the few firms who still build exceptional cars. In the tradition of Frua, Boano and Michelotti or Vignale, the best-known at the present time are Ghia, Bertone, Pininfarina and Italdesign. Each firm consists of a pool of experts in aerodynamics working on computers and a handful of highly skilled artist-designers, whose services are hotly contested. Tom Tjaarda (son of John, who created the Lincoln Zephyr), Paul Bracq, Bruno Sacco, Giorgetto Giugiaro, Franco Sbarro, Gérard Welter, Patrick Le Quément or Wayne Cherry are some of the names most often associated with the design of "concept cars", special automobiles or successful models for the mass market.

Where vehicles for special purposes are concerned, specialized workshops, for example Heuliez in France, work in conjunction with the constructors. There are also specialized enterprises – some big, some small, some independent, some closely associated with one or more marques – which produce kits or replicas. Franco Sbarro is a typical example.

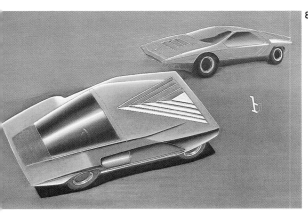

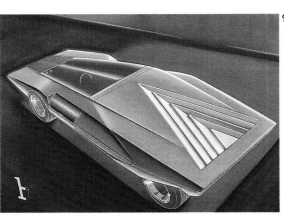

Pininfarina

Some typical designs: the 1990 Alfa Romeo Spyder (2); Citröen Maserati (3); the 1975 Lancia Monte-Carlo (5 and 7).

Bertone

NSU (1); Fiat (4); interior of the 1969 BMW 2800 (6); "Rainbow" 308 GT on a Ferrari platform (11); sketches and designs (8, 9 and 12); Alfa Romeo Carabo, 1969 (13), Navajo, 1977 (14) and Trapèze (15); Fiat 130 coupé (10).

RECORD BREAKERS AND DRAGSTERS

From the very early days of motor racing, speed records have been a constant source of fascination. The most fiercely contested is the world land speed record. Until November 1964, this was restricted to vehicles with a conventional propulsion system. Jet-engined machines were not recognized, because power was not transmitted via the wheels. The regulations have since been amended, with four categories of vehicle now able to compete:

a) land vehicle: a means of locomotion driven by its own source of power, constantly in contact with the ground, either directly, via a mechanical carrying system, or indirectly; means of propulsion and steering controlled entirely and at all times by a driver on board the vehicle;

b) automobile: a vehicle travelling on at least four non-aligned wheels, constantly in contact with the ground;

c) special vehicle: a vehicle with at least four wheels, but not propelled via the wheels;

d) ground effects vehicle: a vehicle which travels on a cushion of pressurized air.

The first recognized speed record was set in 1898 by the Comte de Chasseloup-Laubat driving a Jeantaud electrically powered vehicle at 39.51 mph. The 1,000kph (625 mph) barrier was broken in 1970 by Gary Gabelich in Blue Flame. Stan Barrett reached 743.98 mph aboard the 48,000 hp Budweiser Rocket in 1979, but this attempt was not officially recognized.

The home of dragster racing is the United States. In collaboration with the American Hot Rod Association, the NHRA organizes over 3,000 annual events, at which dragsters of different types race side by side over a quarter of a mile, attempting to out-accelerate each other. Similar competitions are organized in Europe and Australia.

Donald Campbell's Bluebird, which reached a speed of 431.8 mph (1).

The record-breaking 45-litre Sunbeam, which Seagrave drove to over 200 mph in 1927.

Different types of dragster powered by different kinds of fuel (2, 4, 6, 7, 10, 12 and 14), and even by a jet engine (9).

The famous Budweiser Rocket, designed by W. Fredrick. It was propelled by a 48,000 hp rocket engine, while a supplementary lateral rocket supplied an additional 3 tons of thrust! (3).

A record-breaking Alfa Romeo Abarth (5).

The 1957 MG EX 181 (8).

The start of a dragster race (13).

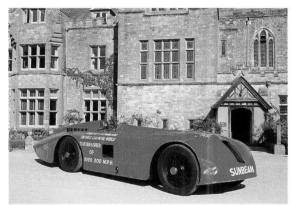

AMPHIBIOUS VEHICLES
BUGGIES • MATRA BAGHEERA
MERCEDES CIII

As well as working to make cars faster and more beautiful, man has always sought to broaden the automobile's field of application. Hence the curiosities grouped together in this section.

One dream has been to create a truly **amphibious vehicle**, able to function as well in the water as on land. (The word comes from the Greek *amphibios*, meaning double life). Although prototypes had already appeared in the early years of the century, it was the military needs of World War II which gave a boost to this area of research. The most notable result was the Volkswagen Schwimmwagen of 1942, which had a fold-away propeller and was similar in looks to the classic Beetle. No marque has got very far in realizing the dream of an all-in-one car and boat, though the Amphicar, built by the German DWM group in the years 1959 to 1969 achieved a degree of success. Similarly, the development of a combined car and aeroplane, such as the highly-imaginative turbine-powered Firebird of 1956, has proved something of a chimera.

Coming down to earth with a bump, the bug-like **buggy** has enjoyed considerable success, in parallel with the development of all-terrain vehicles. Buggies first appeared in the United States in the 1960s and have since become popular worldwide. Originally intended for negotiating sand dunes, they are generally built on a Volkswagen chassis. Of simple design, they are easy to maintain and repair and, because of their natural sporting qualities, have quickly found their niche as leisure cars.

Another exceptional vehicle, though appealing to a quite different public, was the **Bagheera**, built by **Matra** – a company better known for its missiles and Formula 1 racing machines. A car with three front seats, the Bagheera achieved enormous success following its launch in 1973. Similar acclaim should have been enjoyed by the **Mercedes CIII**, a futuristic prototype unveiled by the German marque in 1970. In looks, the car was twenty years ahead of its time, but unfortunately it was never marketed.

Amphibious vehicles

The wartime Volkswagen Schwimmwagen and a close-up of its propeller (3 and 4); the Amphicar, 1965 (1 and 6); an Argoat vehicle (9, 12 and 13).

Buggies

Two shots of buggies in their natural surroundings (5 and 8).

Dream cars

The 1956 Firebird II, a turbine-powered vehicle (2); the 1973 Matra Bagheera (10 and 11); the 1970 Mercedes CIII (7 and 13); two cars that were later developed by body-builders or inventors: the Lancia Fulvia (14), which Ghia modified out of all recognition, and the Chrysler New Yorker (16).

A BEVY OF SMALL CARS

Why not replace the car's petrol tank with batteries? For years this question has given engineers and inventors something to chew on. After all, the railways – the first modern means of transport, which set in motion the nineteenth-century industrial revolution – have given a good example of electric power. Alas! In spite of many attempts to apply the principle to cars, and notwithstanding the oil crisis of the 1970s, which concentrated the minds of manufacturers, the electric car has rarely progressed beyond the experimental stage. There has always been a major stumbling block: the weight of the batteries and the disproportionate amount of space they take up.

On the subject of very small cars which depart from the accepted norm, it is worth mentioning modern three-wheelers. These include the British Reliant; the remarkable Isetta, a front-opening bubble-car built by BMW in the mid-1950s to an Italian design; utility vehicles of all kinds; and the contemporary small-engined "minis", such as the Ligier, which combine the virtues of car and motorbike in heavy urban traffic. A word must also be said for the Trabant, a small car typifying the popular mass culture of East Germany.

Established in 1955 with the backing of Fiat and Pirelli, the Italian Autobianchi company has been one of the foremost producers of small cars: from the Blanchina, launched to great acclaim in 1957, to the AIII, which made its debut in 1967. Shortly before, Fiat had reabsorbed the marque and completely revised its image, but later, more spacious models were not nearly so successful.

Best known for commercial vehicles and trucks (which it began making in 1949), in the late 1950s the Dutch Daf company began turning out small cars, all of which were fitted with automatic transmission. Its first venture was the Daffodil, launched in 1959. This was followed, in 1966-67, by the 33, 44 and 55 range of models, and, in the mid-1970s, by the 66.

Battery-powered cars
13 The Comuta, built by Ford in 1967 (5 and 6).

Autobianchi
The 1971 A112 (14); the 1965 Primula (12 and 15).

Daf
The 33, 44 and 55 models, dating from 1966-67 (7, 13 and 9).

Miscellaneous
The Reliant Robin (2 and 3); the BMW Isetta (4); a Ligier "mini car" (1); a wooden-bodied Hustler (10); and two East German Trabants (8 and 11).

ALL-TERRAIN VEHICLES

In terms of volume, all-terrain vehicles occupy only a small part of the motor car market. But, with the growth of leisure activities and the popularity of rallies like the Paris-Dakar, 4x4 or 4WD models – as they are more commonly referred to – have gained enormous prestige. Fashion has also played a large part in their success: though designed to tackle the most arduous conditions, they are in fact frequently used for getting about town.

Nowadays, all the major manufacturers list all-terrain vehicles in their catalogues. Some of the more prestigious marques have also entered the field, for instance Lamborghini with the LM 002 – a 450 hp monster whose engine is derived from the Countach's V12. But the real specialists are the Japanese: Toyota, Nissan, Mitsubishi, Isuzu and Suzuki. Their target is not just top-of-the-range customers in prosperous countries, but the far wider market for combined road transport and utility vehicles in the many parts of the world with sub-standard road networks: from the Sahara to the Australian outback, from the American West to rugged mountain regions. The most successful of these Japanese models have been the Mitsubishi Pajero (which has performed amazingly on the road and in African rallies) and the Toyota Land Cruisers, used worldwide since 1954.

Of the traditional makes, the most prestigious is still Land Rover, which the British company has chosen to maintain as a separate entity. With its Land Rovers, Range Rovers and the new Discovery, the marque produces over 50,000 4x4 vehicles a year.

Some countries whose car industries are not generally esteemed have made their best efforts in the field of all-terrain vehicles. This is true of Portugal (Portaro, UMM), Romania (Aro), the former USSR (Lada), and Spain (Santana). American marques, on the other hand, have tended to miss the 4x4 bus, dissipating their energies in a plethora of different models.

Toyota
Land Cruiser (1); a turbo version (9); and a pick-up (12).

Daihatsu
Sportrack EFI (2).

Mercedes
300 GE (3).

Land Rover
Land Rover (6, 7, 10 and 14), Range Rover (11) and the Discovery (4).

Mitsubishi
The long-wheelbase Pajero during the Paris-Dakar rally (8); Shogun V6 (19).

Lamborghini
LM 002 4x4 (5).

Isuzu
Trooper (13).

Suzuki
Vitara (15, 17 and 18).

Santana
Santana (16).

Nissan
A Patrol entered for the Paris-Dakar event (20).

CARS FROM EASTERN EUROPE, ASIA AND ELSEWHERE

Some makes of car, though not generally well known, are widely used in certain countries or parts of the world, where they often cater to a captive market.

Although in India many of the vehicles on the road are ancient British or Italian models, some home-produced makes have recently made their appearance, such as Hindustan, Premier, Maru uti, Sipani, Trishul and Mahindra-Jeep.

In Australia, Ford dominates the market, producing a number of specific models at its Homebush plant in Sydney. The Holden company, which began life in 1926 as a subsidiary of General Motors and in 1931 joined Holden's Body Builders Ltd to form G.M.H., introduced its first specific model in November 1948.

In Asia, the Chinese produce cars at Beijing and Shanghai, and South Korea is also developing its automobile industry thanks to Daewo Motor and Hyundai. The latter was set up in 1967.

Eastern Europe has produced many of its cars under licence. Notable examples are Lada – known in the former USSR as Zhiguli – and Zavasta-Yugo in Yugoslavia, whose plants were installed by Fiat. Russian manufacturers include Moskvitch, Ij and Volga-Gaz. Now that free trade has opened up with the West, FSM and FSO-Polski in Poland and Skoda and Tatra in Czechoslovakia are in danger of losing their markets, as has already happened with Trabant and Wartburg in the former German Democratic Republic.

While on the subject of curiosities, there have been some interesting limited editions: for instance, the short-lived but very Spanish Pegaso models. More recently, the company has concentrated exclusively on commercial vehicles.

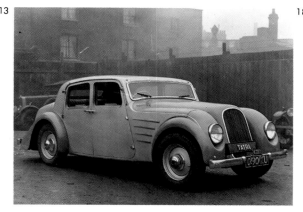

Skoda
Cars from Czechoslovakia: the Estelle 139 Sport (1), and the Favorit 136 'Estate' (12).

Lada-Vaz
Built with help from Fiat at Togliattigrad in 1969, Lada-Vaz is the biggest Russian manufacturer of private cars (2 and 10).

Pegaso
Spanish models: the 1953 Z 102 (3), and the 56/58 (8).

Australian models
The locally-produced Ford Falcon (4); the Australian Six, dating from 1918 (5); the Holden Brougham (7), and a much earlier 1963 version (11).

Mahindra
The Indian company's Chief (6).

Tatra
The Czech company's V8 77, dating from 1935 (9 and 13); and a 1934 model (18).

Yugo
The Tempo (14) and Sana (15).

Hyundai
The South Korean marque's Stellar 1600 SC (16) and Sonata 2.0i (17).

MADE IN ENGLAND

ASTON MARTIN

With Frazer-Nash and Lagonda, **Aston Martin** produced the finest – and most expensive – British sports cars of the pre-war era. The firm was established in 1922 by Lionel Martin. The Aston part of the name is explained by the fact that Martin had won the Aston-Clinton hill-climb race in 1913. The marque soon came to the fore in motor racing, competing nine times at Le Mans in the years 1928 to 1939. And success on the race track won Aston Martin the loyalty of a demanding and wealthy clientele.

Unfortunately, the company's brilliant results in motor sport were not matched by its financial performance. Aston Martin was on the verge of bankruptcy when, in early 1947, David Brown stepped in, buying out both Aston Martin and Lagonda. Heir to an industrial dynasty specializing in the manufacture of agricultural tractors, Brown breathed new life into the marque, while maintaining its sporting tradition. The DB 1 and DB 2 (1950-1959) models were followed by a true racing car: the DB 3. The DB 4, a prestigious touring model brought out in 1958, presented a serious challenge to Ferrari. In response to the Italian marque's 250 GT, David Brown introduced the DB 4 GT, a 6-cylinder machine developing over 300 hp, then the GT Zagato and the Vantage. Next came the DB 5 and DB 6, immortalized as the favourite cars of agent 007 James Bond.

With the advent of the V8 engine, Aston Martin cars lost something of their sporting glamour, but it was the oil crisis that proved fatal, driving the company out of business in 1974. The Newport Pagnell firm was rescued a year later by two North American industrialists. In recent times, Aston Martin has produced a range of large, high-performance coupés. These include the V8 Saloon, the Volante and the Vantage, with such variants as the Lagonda and the Vantage Zagato.

Aston Martin V8 (1).
A 1961 example of the DB 2 Volante (2 and 5).
The DB S, 1967 (3).
Aston Martin DB 4 (4).
A 1970 version of the DB 6 II Vantage (6).
The uncharacteristic Bulldog (11 and 16).
The DB 4 Volante (7).
Aston Martin D Type (8).
The DB 5 Volante, introduced in 1964 (9).
Coachwork by Zagato (10).
Aston Martin DB 5 (12).
A DB 2 Saloon of 1952 vintage (13).
The 1985 version of the Vantage (14).
A 1932 model from the Lionel Martin era (15).
The 1953 DB 3 (17).

PREVIOUS PAGES: Aston Martin V8. Insets: a Lotus turbo SE; and a 1948 Triumph roadster.

DAIMLER

I n 1890 there were only four major automobile constructors: Benz, **Daimler**, Panhard-Levassor and Peugeot. During the last decade of the century, the New York piano manufacturer William Steinway acquired the right to use designs patented by Gottfried Daimler, and this was the birth of the American car industry. Subsidiaries of the German Daimler company proliferated, giving rise in the early 1900s to such organizations as Austro-Daimler and British-Daimler. The parent company eventually merged with Benz in 1926.

In the early part of the century, British Daimler concentrated on building a succession of fast, heavy sports cars. During the 1930s, Daimler was the official supplier of limousines to the royal family but lost ground to some extent as competition in the luxury car sector intensified. The firm nevertheless maintained its prestige and vitality, constantly renewing its range and adapting to the requirements of a loyal clientele of wealthy customers. Special commissions were always honoured. The last model introduced before World War II was the Light 15 Saloon, while the immediate post-war models were the DE 36 (1947) and the Empress. The late 1950s saw the arrival of the SP 250 roadster, powered by a V8 engine. The SP 250 was the marque's last true sports car. Subsequently, Daimler was absorbed by the British Leyland group, and the name has since been applied to luxury versions of the Jaguar XJ series, which sport the traditional Daimler radiator grill. There still remains one authentic Daimler, however: the DS 420 limousine, used on state and ceremonial occasions, which was introduced in 1968. Though somewhat outmoded in appearance, it is the successor of a noble line of cars.

A 1910 Daimler 15 hp (1 and 6).

The 1960 Daimler SP 250 Dart (2, 5).

The Empress saloon, 1953 (3).

A 1974 version of the Daimler Double-Six V12 (4).

The 1939 Light 15 Saloon (7)

The Daimler 2.5-litre V8 250.

The Daimler DB 18 (9).

Daimler drophead coupé, 1934 (10).

The DE 36 ST8, introduced in 1947 (14).

The 1899 Daimler 12 hp Royal (12).

An 1898 Canstatt Daimler (13).

This Daimler, finished in silver, was built for tiger hunting in 1926 (15 and 16).

The Daimler Docker (17).

AC • AUSTIN-HEALEY • MG

Founded in 1904, the Thames Ditton firm Autocars & Accessories Ltd became Autocarriers in 1911, and **AC** Cars Ltd in 1927. Two years later, the marque was acquired by the Hurlock brothers, who produced the three-seater Magna, then a series of two-seater saloons and roadsters. The AC ACE, introduced in October 1953, was the first British car with independent suspension. In 1956, the sports car specialist Ken Rudd persuaded the Hurlocks to equip their roadster with the Bristol 2-litre engine. The ACE Bristol was a great success, but the firm suffered a severe setback in 1961, when Bristol stopped producing its 6-cylinder engine. AC then turned to Ford. At the same time, the American Caroll Shelby, knowing AC to be in difficulty, suggested that he produce and market a derivative. As a result, in 1962 Shelby American introduced the Cobra 260, with a production run of 75. The following year, the 289 version – again powered by a V8 engine – was credited with a top speed of 168 mph. Then came the famous AC Cobra 427: a 425 hp monster with phenomenal acceleration, available in racing and "street" versions. The 427 was withdrawn in late 1966. The 285 hp 289 continued in production until 1969, when AC went bankrupt, leaving a few enthusiasts to produce replicas of its legendary roadster.

A former mechanic with a passion for the race track, Donald Mitchell Healey joined Triumph as its technical director in 1933. While developing tanks with the Humber company during the war, he met three other talented engineers. This team was encouraged by the firm's Hereford dealer, who let them use his premises to build two prototypes: a roadster – the Westland – which was ready in early 1946, and a hardtop – the Elliot – which was finished later in the year. Donald Healey had built the fastest sports car in England, with a top speed of 103 mph. Powered by a Nash engine, it had a distinguished racing career.

In reply to competition from the Jaguar XK 120, Healey sought help from BMC, who supplied the Austin A 90 engine, and the designer Coker. The result was the **Austin-Healey** 100, which first emerged from Austin's Longbridge assembly works in 1952. The first five cars has aluminium bodywork, but production began in earnest the following year, when a steel body was fitted. The 100 was followed by the Sprite, then the MkI and MkII series and the 3000 MkIII – the "Big Healey" – 17,712 of which were produced in four years. New American regulations sounded the death knell of this model, 80 per cent of the production run having been marketed in the United States.

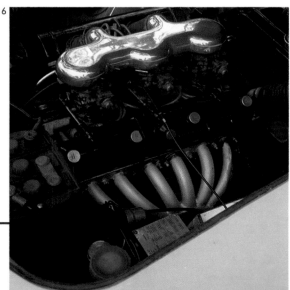

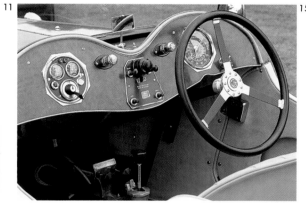

In the 1920s, Cecil Kimber and Morris Garages of Oxford had promoted stylish sports cars for hair-in-the-wind enthusiasts under the name of **MG**. The Midget and Magnette were typical of their philosophy: small, responsive, streamlined and affordable, being built from modified standard components. The success of the two-seater M-Types, J2s, PAs and PBs was continued by the MGT (1936-1955) and, in the early 1950s, the thirties-style bodywork of the TC made it an excellent ambassador for British cars in the USA. But it was after 1955, with the advent of the superb MGA and its descendants – the MGB, MGB-GT, MGC (with production figures in excess of 500,000 over an eighteen-year period) – that the Abingdon marque really became universally known. The company was subsequently absorbed by the Austin-Rover group. The latest car to bear the MG insignia is a sports version of the Metro, the 6R4.

AC

The AC 3000 ME V6, presented in October 1973 after a long and difficult period of gestation (1).
The 1959 AC Greyhound, with close-up of engine (2 and 6).
Autokraft's AC Cobra: a replica of the Shelby-built monster (3).
Under the aegis of Portwine and Weller, this AC was introduced by Autocarriers in 1921 (4).
The AC Cobra 427 (5).

Austin-Healey

The Sprite, 1958 (7 and 11).
A 1960 version of the Austin-Healey 3000 MkI (12).
Austin-Healey 3000 MkII (8).

MG

The MG Midget (9 and 13)
The 1930 MG "M" type (14)
The dashboard of a 1934 PA
An MGA 1600 MkII roadster of 1962 vintage (10).

ROVER • TRIUMPH
LOTUS • MARCOS

The name **Rover** dates back to 1884, when it was given to a front-wheel-drive tricycle conceived by John K. Starley and William Sutton, who together had founded a workshop in Coventry in 1877. The first Rover motor car, designed by E.W. Lewis, was an 8 hp model introduced in 1904. The company entered a phase of expansion, eventually producing 17,000 of the cars. After 1918 the business, which had been prominent in the war effort, moved to a small factory in Birmingham. In 1924 the Rover 14/45 hp was awarded the Dewar Trophy, the highest accolade of the Royal Automobile Club. In 1933 a new manager, Spencer B. Wilks, centralized all the company's production facilities in Birmingham, and aimed for high standards of "comfort, performance and refinement". After World War II, in which the company again played an active role, Rover moved to new premises in Solihull, where in 1947 it brought out the P2, soon followed by the P3, P4 and P5 series. It also developed the Land Rover, which made its debut in 1948.

British sports cars rapidly achieved prominence in the immediate post-war years, and sold particularly well in the United States. To match MG, in 1950 **Triumph** launched its TR series. Three TRX prototypes were followed by the TR 1 (introduced in 1952); then by the TR 2 (53-55); the TR 3 and TR 3A (55-62); the TR 4, presented in 1962, with bodywork by Michelotti; the TR 4A; the 6-cylinder TR 5 and TR 250 series; and the Karmann-designed TR 6 and GT6 models. Twenty thousand TRs were produced in all, mostly for export to the USA. Another highly successful model was the competitively priced Spitfire, 314,000 of which were sold in the years 1962 to 1976.

The first **Lotus** was the Seven, an experimental machine designed by Colin Bruce Chapman in 1948. The Lotus company was founded in 1951 to build Formula racing cars, and in 1957 also began marketing Gran Turismo models. In April 1986, the business was taken over by General Motors.

The **Marcos** company specialized in styling racing versions of the Mini Cooper. Its own models made a brief appearance in the years 1962 to 1966. Early examples of the final Marcos model, the 1600 GT Mantula coupé, were fitted with a Volvo engine, later superseded by a Ford power unit.

Rover

Rover 9 hp of 1909 (1).
A 1960 Rover (8).
A Rover 2000 model of 1967 (11)
The Rover "Turbine" (14).
The Rover 6-cylinder "Cyclops" of 1950 (15).

Triumph

Triumph Herald 1200 coupé (5).
1959 examples of the Triumph TR 3 A (9 and 13).
A 1954 TR 2 (7 and 10).

Lotus

A recent version of the Lotus Esprit (2).
A Lotus Elan of 1972 vintage (3).
The 1978 version of the Lotus Esprit (4).
Lotus Esprit Turbo SE (6).

Marcos

Last of the breed: the Marcos Mantula (12).

JAGUAR

The **Jaguar** story begins with two motorcycle enthusiasts from Blackpool, William Lyons and Bill Walmsley, who in 1922 began making and selling sidecars. By 1926, the Swallow Sidecar and Coach Building Co. was making car bodies for Morris, Austin and Wolseley. Two years later the firm, renamed SSD, moved to Coventry, where it produced its first complete car in 1931. The constant aim was to achieve the best possible quality-price ratio.

The company recruited top-class engineers, and in 1935 the introduction of the SS 100 marked the advent of large-scale production methods. At about this time Bill Walmsley was declared bankrupt, leaving William Lyons to go it alone.

After the war, with British industry picking up the pieces, Sir Williams Lyons stopped making military equipment and looked for a way of relaunching his business. The British government was offering generous subsidies to firms manufacturing for the American market. The SS initials, with their unhappy connotations, were abandoned, and on 3 March 1945 the leaping Jaguar made its first official appearance, as Lyons launched his project to produce a fast luxury car that would sell in the States. The XK 120 (top speed 120 mph), was the first of a new generation of models. At the same time, aware that involvement in motor racing was vital as a way of demonstrating the marque's prowess, Lyons brought out parallel sports car versions: the C and D types, corresponding to the XK 140 (1954) and XK 150 (1957) saloons. The sports car series culminated, in 1961, in the revolutionary E Type, hot from the race track, which was fitted with disc brakes on all four wheels.

The E Type was the last of its kind: a beautiful car at an affordable price. The final version was marketed in 1975. In the meantime, a new generation of cars had appeared, combining wood and leather with plastic, and with electronic injection: the XJS range, which was never to

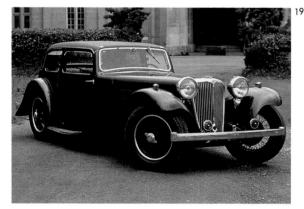

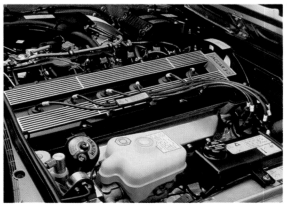

produce its "F Type". On the saloon car side, the 2.4 and 3.4 were superseded by the Mark 2 (production figures: 100,000) and a whole range of successors. The 1961 Mark X was a whale of a car, which, after a lot of work in the wind tunnel, resulted in the slimmed down XJ, first introduced in 1964. The XJ series really began to sell in 1969, when the XJ 6 was voted "Car of the Year".

Still active in motor sport, this British marque nowadays occupies a secure niche in the upper reaches of the luxury sports car market.

The S-type saloon (1).
This Sovereign model is powered by a 4-litre engine (2).
The Jaguar Mk VII (3).
First of the post-war generation: the XK 120 (4 and 9).
The XK 140, dating from 1954 (5).
Big-engined cars: the XJR 6.0 and the 6.0 S (6, 10, 13 and 17).
The XJ 220 model (7 and 14)
The XK 150 (8).
Illustrations of the XJ6 and its 3.2-litre engine (11, 12, 15 and 16).
The SS 100, introduced in 1935, marked the beginning of large-scale production (18).
The 1931 SS1 (19).

DISTINGUISHING MARQUES

FORD

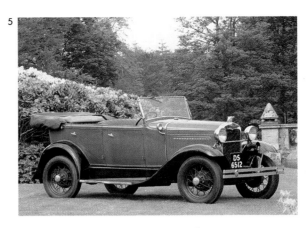

With an annual production figure of five-and-a-half-million vehicles, the American-based marque, which ranks second in the world, remains faithful to the tradition inaugurated in 1903 by its brilliant founder. Son of an Irish immigrant who had settled in Michigan, Henry **Ford** was born in 1861. He had virtually no formal schooling, and at the age of sixteen left the family farm to seek his fortune in the engineering workshops of Detroit. The archetypal self-made man, he designed his first engine in 1887 and his first automobile – a prototype that was never marketed – in 1896. In 1903 he finally founded his own company. His first great achievement was the Model T, more than fifteen million of which were produced. This was the ancestor of a great line of cars – including such striking models as the Thunderbird (restyled over and again since 1955) and the Mustang (six million sold since 1964) – which has continued long after Henry Ford's retirement, in 1927, and eventual death, in April 1947. Ford was also one of the first to understand that the future of companies such as his own depended on their automobiles being manufactured and marketed worldwide. He accordingly established Ford of Britain in 1911, a German subsidiary in 1920, and associated companies in Brazil and Mexico in 1925, and quickly built up an international reputation. The overseas branches of Ford were soon designing models of their own: the Anglia, Zodiac, Consul and Cortina in the UK; the Taunus and Escort in Germany; the Vendôme and Vedette in France. Nowadays, more than half of Ford's annual output of 5.5 million vehicles is manufactured outside the United States, with Europe accounting for 1.6 million of the total. The most popular Ford models at the present time are the Escort, which dates from 1967; the Sierra, introduced in 1982, the sports version of which has done brilliantly in rallying; and, to a lesser extent, the Fiesta.

Models designed by Ford of Britain: a 1949 Anglia (1); a 1963 Consul-Cortina estate (2); a Consul Classic Capri (7); a 3-litre Capri with bodywork by Ghia (8); and a 1964 Cortina MK1 (17). 1975 and 1987 examples of the Taunus (3 and 15), the highly successful model first produced by Ford of Germany in 1962. The German company later introduced the Escort, a 1983 1.3-litre version of which is shown here (4).

Some older models: model A Phaeton, 1930 (5); Tudor De Luxe, 1941 (6); Fairline, 1955 (16).

The Thunderbird: a 1957 model (12); the 1987 turbo version (9).

A Sierra RS 500 Cosworth, 1987 (10 and 13); a 1989 Fiesta (14); and a Granada Scorpio 4x4 (11).

PREVIOUS PAGES: the Lancia Delta Integrale. Insets, left: Mitsubishi Colt and Renault Clio; right, top to bottom: Ford Sierra 4x4, Rover Sterling and HM the Queen's sixteen-valve Saab 900 Turbo.

FIAT

At the end of the 1980s, **Fiat** was selling an average of just over 2.3 million vehicles a year, making it a close second to Volkswagen among European automobile manufacturers. As, over the years, the Fiat group has acquired other marques – Lancia, Alfa Romeo, Ferrari and, more recently, Innocenti and a substantial stake in Maserati – it has come to have a near-hegemony of Italian car production.

It was in 1899 that Giovanni Agnelli, first in a long line of entrepreneurs whose descendants still control the business, decided to begin manufacturing motor cars. His company, Fabbrica Italiana Automobili Torino, immediately became known by its initials: F.I.A.T. He first marketed a 3.5 hp model, but it was not until 1912, with the Zero series, that Fiat really achieved success. This was the beginning of the company's orientation towards popular, mass-produced cars, which continued with the 501, introduced in 1918, and the celebrated 500, or "Topolino", launched in 1936.

Designed by Dante Giocosa, the Topolino (which means mouse) made Fiat famous. The idea was to offer a miniature saloon, capable of transporting two people and their luggage over long distances as inexpensively as possible. The Topolino has had many successors, and today the concept lives on in the Panda. Fiat now offers a complete range of cars: Panda, Uno, Tipo, Tempra and Croma. To these must be added the many models produced by the other marques which now form part of the group. Most of these have a sporting pedigree, continuing Fiat's long-standing involvement in motor racing – a field in which the marque has had a glorious history in its own right.

The 1905 100 hp (3).

The SB4: specially built in response to an American challenge in 1908 (5).

The 1913 Tipo Zero (10).

Early versions of the Topolino, dating from 1936 and 1937 (2 and 4).

The 1967 Dino (11).

The Abarth 1600, 1969 (6).

The 126, dating from 1972 (7).

Three incarnations of the 124: the 1972 standard model (13), a spyder version (12), and the 1970 Sport Coupé (16).

The 127, 1977 vintage (8).

From Fiat's current range: the Uno (1), the Croma (9), the Tipo (4) and the Tempra (15).

LANCIA

Although the history of **Lancia**, going back nearly a century, is somewhat fragmented, the marque has always embodied a typically Italian tradition of high-class automobile engineering, producing a large number of responsive and stylish models.

It was in 1906 that Vincenzo Lancia, who had enjoyed a brilliant racing career with Fiat, decided to set up his own company. His first model, the 18/24 hp, came out the following year. It soon became known as the Alfa, inaugurating the marque's long tradition of naming its cars with letters of the Greek alphabet. But the legendary model of this first period in Lancia's history, which ended with the death of its founder in 1937, was undoubtedly the Lambda. Other extremely popular models in the 1930s were the Augusta and the Aprilia, two compact saloon cars of the highest quality. Lancia then put much of its effort into motor racing, and the marque's experience in this field was invaluable in promoting its recovery in the early 1970s, as it embarked on the third phase of its career.

Two key dates in Lancia's recent history were 1969, when the marque became part of the Fiat group, and 1971, which saw the arrival of the Stratos, a car which was to dominate rallying for almost a decade. Lancia's association with Fiat brought about a profound change, particularly on the sales front. The first model of the Fiat era was the Beta, unveiled in 1972, soon to be followed by a complete new range.

Lancia's main models today are the nippy little Y10, the comfortable Dedra and Thema saloons and, if you are looking for performance, the magnificent Delta Integrale. This car has won many honours in the last few years in such top-level events as the Monte Carlo and Argentine Rallies, the Safari and the Tour of Corsica.

7 Some historic models: the Augusta, dating from 1934 (6), the Aprilia, 1938 (1), and the 1964 Flamina Saloon (2). The current Delta range: a 1988 Z4LX 1300 (5), a 1991 HF Integrale (8 and 9), LX and GT (11 and 12), and the diminutive Y10 (3). The Thema LX Turbo (4), and the 16-valve version (10). The Dedra 2000 Turbo (7).

ALFA ROMEO

Since its foundation in 1909, Alfa (which stands for Anonima Lombarda Fabbrica Automobili) has always maintained an extremely high profile, especially on the race track. The story begins with a Frenchman, Alexandre Darracq, one of the pioneers of the automobile industry, who set up car assembly plants in Naples and just outside Milan. His enterprise did not prosper, however, and he eventually sold his Lombardy workshops to a consortium of local businessmen. They in turn appointed Ing. Giuseppe Merosi – an employee of Darracq's – to produce cars under the Alfa name. Darracq's double "D" was replaced by the emblem which ever since has adorned Alfa cars: the red cross of the Milanese crusaders and the biblical serpent which featured on their banners in medieval times. To this double symbol was later added a blue surround with the marque's new name of **Alfa-Romeo**, after Nicola Romeo, a Milanese industrialist, had bought out the existing company in 1915.

From the very beginning Alfa showed a propensity for making fast cars, and this tradition has always been maintained. The reputation for speed has been confirmed by the marque's true racing cars – from the legendary early models designed by Merosi in the 1920s to the single-seater Grand Prix machines of the 1950s – and by the standard production vehicles it produced at the small Lombard town of Portello. Throughout Alfa's history there has always been a close link between the marque's standard models and its racing cars. Sadly, in recent years, Alfa has virtually abandoned top competition: since the marque became part of the Fiat group in 1986, the sporting role has been largely taken over by its sister companies Lancia and Ferrari.

The honourable tradition established in the 1950s and '60s by the many versions of the Giulietta is nevertheless perpetuated by Alfa's current models, especially the 75 and 164 ranges. At the same time, the 33 is the expression of a policy adopted in the 1970s, when the company set up plants in the South of Italy and produced cars under the name of Alfasud. The finest car now bearing the Alfa-Romeo emblem is undoubtedly its Spyder model, first introduced in 1966 with bodywork by the great Pininfarina. This magnificent cabriolet embodies all the outstanding virtues of the marque.

The Alfa 33: a 1.5-litre model dating from 1984 (4 and 11), and a 16-valve 1.7-litre version (5 and 12); its forerunner, the Alfasud: two models of 1982 vintage (9 and 10).

Interior of the Alfa 75 (2).

The Alfa 164, 1989 version (6).

The Spider: the 1600 version dating from 1974 (3), and the 1990 Pininfarina edition (7).

The ES 30 Coupé, unveiled at the Geneva Motor Show in 1988 (1 and 8).

RENAULT

Louis Renault – the fourth of six children – did not do well at school, to the mortification of his father, a rich draper of Billancourt, then still a rural suburb of late nineteenth-century Paris. His mind was filled, instead, with thoughts of locomotives and other machines – symbols of the amazing technical progress of the times. At sixteen he was spending his time stripping down and reassembling the family Panhard, and making his own modifications to a variety of engines. Alone in the workshop at the bottom of the garden, applying the knowledge he had acquired by experience, he invented a system of direct-drive transmission, effectively the first modern gearbox. His brother Michel collaborated in fitting this innovation to a quadricycle he had just made. The result was the first **Renault**; the year 1898.

With the aid of their father, who did not need much convincing, Louis and two of his brothers set up a firm in the family name to manufacture vehicles of this kind. Since then, the Billancourt marque has always been in the forefront of the French motor car industry. More than that, it has played a central role in the nation's life, as when six hundred Renault taxis were used to transport troops to the Battle of the Marne in September 1914, helping to bring victory out of defeat. It used to be said that: "When Billancourt caught a cold, all of France sneezed". Such has been the company's economic importance, both under the rule of Louis Renault, who died in 1944, and since the war, as a nationalized industry.

Renault cars have always been characterized by their simplicity, in the right sense of the word. Some outstanding models over the years have included the 40 CV of the 1920s, a high-class, long-bodied limousine; the 1948 4 CV, a superb little popular car; the round-winged Fregate-Dauphines and Florides of the 1950s; and the R4 or 4L and its successors, the R5 and the Clio. A recent addition to the family is the R19, a middle-of-the-range model at a

12 reasonable price, which has won international acclaim and done much to restore the company's fortunes at a difficult time.

A 1911 AX (5).
The post-war 4 CV (2).
A 1954 Fregate Affair (3).
The Dauphine, dating from 1960 (6). Gordini versions of the R8, R12 (1971) and R17 (1976) (1, 4 and 7).
A 1962 example of the Floride (8).
A 1975 4L (10).
From the current range of models: 3 and 5-door versions of the Clio (13), the R19 GTS (12), the R20 (14), the R25 (15 and 16), the Alpine GTA (9) and the V6 Turbo (11).

PEUGEOT

The Peugeots were an enterprising family who, as far back as the late 1700s, had begun to make the area around Montbelliard – in the Franche-Comté region of eastern France – one of the cradles of France's industrial revolution. With a tradition of steel foundries, rolling mills, coffee grinders and bicycles behind them, it was inevitable that one day a son of the family would launch out into automobile manufacture. That son was Armand **Peugeot**. His first effort was a steam driven tricycle, presented at the 1889 Universal Exhibition – some years before he founded the Société des Automobiles Peugeot in 1896. His first workshops were in the Paris area, but eventually the Sochaux factory, near Montbelliard, became the headquarters and showpiece of the company.

The Type 81 and 91 Torpedoes of the early years were promising machines, but Peugeot's first great success came in the early 1920s with the Quadrilette, followed by the 201, which won the Monte Carlo Rally at its first attempt in 1931. Its descendants were the 301 and 401 models and the streamlined 6-cylinder 601, introduced in 1934. Then began a second series of cars, the 402 winning at Le Mans in 1938.

Peugeot has since maintained its happy tradition of giving each new model a three-figure designation: the first now indicates the range (levels 1 to 6), the second is always a zero, while the third records the successive generations of a given model (the 1990s have seen the birth of a sixth). Each generation has produced its star: the 203 in the immediate post-war period; the incomparable 404, indestructible queen of the African bush; and the 205, one of the great cars of the 1980s, which has helped the marque emerge triumphant from the identity crisis affecting the car industry as a whole.

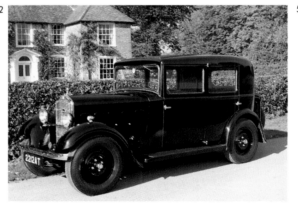

A 301 of 1932 vintage (1).

A Quadrilette 4CV, dating from 1921 (4).

The 201 B, 1933 (2) and a 1930 version of the 201 cabriolet (7).

The 402 B, a 1937 model (5).

The 1959 edition of the 203 saloon (3).

The 204, 1966 (6).

The 404, 1974 (9), 504 cabriolet, 1974 (14), and 104 (13).

The 205 GTI, 1989 (11), 309 GR, 1985 (8), 405 MI16 (12), 506 V6, 1989 (15) and 1990 version of the 605 (10).

CITROEN

André Citroën, a man who combined prodigious intelligence with a fertile imagination, trained as an engineer at the Ecole Polytechnique in Paris. The marque he founded is unquestionably one of the most fascinating in the history of the motor car. Citroën produced unconventional models, and always sought to extend the frontiers of human achievement. This explains the legendary expeditions he organized in the 1920s and '30s: Haardt and Audoin-Dubreuil's crossing of the Sahara in 1923 using tracked vehicles; the famous Africa expedition, which reached Mozambique on 14 June 1925 after crossing the continent from north to south; and the amazing "Croisière Jaune" of 1931-32, covering the 13,000km from Beirut to Peking over incredibly dangerous roads, particularly in the Himalayas. These extraordinary feats were André Citroën's way of proclaiming his faith in the motor car. Citroën himself maintained control of the company until the late 1930s. His faith has been borne out by the many models the marque has created over the years. In discussing the all-time greats, we have already mentioned the Traction, introduced in 1934; the 2CV, conceived before the war but not born until 1948; and the DS19, unveiled in 1955. But we should also bear in mind the C4 and C6 models of the 1930s, the many variants of the DS, the 21, the ID, the Ami 6 (derived form the 2CV), and, in the 1970s, the opulent SM.

In recent years, at a time of far-reaching changes in the world car industry, Citroën has suffered from a lack of foresight in updating its range. New hope of the marque regaining lost ground has come with the introduction of the luxurious XM and, in 1990, the highly successful CX, the sports version of which has been dominating the long-distance African rallies.

A 1966 example of the DS 21 cabriolet (1).

The GS Club (2) and a standard GS of 1971 vintage (5).

Two views of the SM, 1975 (3 and 6).

The Ami 6 and Ami 8 (4 and 7).

The CX long-wheelbase model, 1981 (10).

The BX 19 (11); 16-valve version and close-up of engine (14 and 15).

The AX 14 TGD (8) and AX GT (12).

The XM, introduced in 1990 (13).

A prototype three-wheeler (9).

THE JAPANESE

The Japanese car industry may still be young compared with its counterparts in the United States and Europe, but the dynamism it has shown in recent times has more than made up for its late start.

The first Japanese car – a prototype fitted with an imported American engine – was built in 1902 by engineers Shintaro Yoshida and Komanosuke Uchiyama. In 1907, they turned out the first 100 per cent Japanese automobile, the Takuri, but no more than ten of the cars were produced. A lack of decent roads, natural disasters such as the 1923 earthquake, the country's isolation during the 1930s, then the war, militated against the expansion of the Japanese car industry.

Although Mitsubishi, for whom cars were but one interest among many, had built a four-cylinder machine akin to the Fiat Zero as early as 1917, the group did not begin producing automobiles on a mass scale until the 1960s. The same was true of Mazda, Subaru and Suzuki. Only Nissan and Toyota had made more serious attempts, producing civilian cars in the 1930s. But it was not until the post-war period that the Japanese industry really began to develop. In 1947, for instance, a new company was set up at Suzuka by a brilliant mechanic named Soichiro Honda.

At first, the Japanese companies did no more than imitate their seniors, then, in the 1970s, they began to take over as the driving force behind the world market. Today they have a preponderant influence, despite the imposition of import quotas on their products, particularly in Europe. In all sectors, from the smallest minis to all-terrain vehicles, from family saloons to Formula 1 racing cars, from open-top sports cars (hats off to Mazda's superb Miata!) to pick-ups, the Japanese are present and active, often leading the field. The inexorable Japanese progress is led by Toyota, the world's third biggest car manufacturer, followed by Nissan, Mitsubishi and Honda, Daihatsu (part of the Toyota group), Subaru and Suzuki.

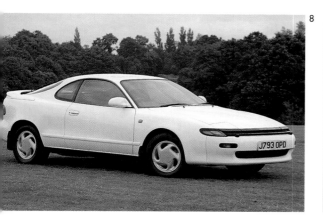

Mazda

1.3-litre LX version of the 121, 1987 (1); 1.8-litre LX version of the 626, 1987 (2); the Miata MX5 (9, 10 and 11).

Honda

Concerto 16l, 1990 (3); an Accord of 1987 vintage (18).

Toyota

Celica GT (5 and 8); 2-litre Celica GT cabriolet, 1988, and engine (6 and 13); MR2, 1990 (4 and 7).

Mitsubishi

Lancer, GTI 16-valve version (12) and 1800 GTI saloon version (15); 1.6-litre Colt turbo, 1987 (14).

Nissan

1.3-litre Sunny LX, 1987 (17); Bluebird ZX turbo, 1988 (16).

VOLVO • SAAB

Sweden's long and honourable tradition in the automotive field today rests on the shoulders of two high-class marques: **Volvo** and **Saab**. The very first Swedish automobile was a motorized quadricycle built in 1894 by an ironmaster, Anders Cederholm. Not until 1926, when the Volvo (from the Latin "I turn") group was founded, did automobile construction provide the powerful Swedish metallurgical industry with the outlet it needed. Volvo also specializes in trucks and industrial vehicles. In the car field, the marque made a name for itself in the late 1940s with its American-inspired PV models. These were followed in the 1950s and 60s, by the P series, the most famous of which were the P 1900, a sports model introduced in 1954, and the long-bodied P 1800, unveiled in 1960, with coachwork by the Italian Pietro Frua. Nowadays, Volvo is a multi-national concern, having bought out Daf of Holland and formed an alliance with Renault. Its cars, such as the wide range of 700 models introduced in 1982, are renowned for robustness and reliability.

Svenska Aeroplan AB, better known as SAAB, was founded in 1937 to produce military aircraft. Not until 1949 did Saab enter the automotive field, initially producing small cars inspired by the German DKWs. Its sports versions having tasted success in rallying, the marque began to concentrate on up-market models, all with characteristically rounded lines. The name for safety and reliability enjoyed by today's magnificent 900 and 9000 models has been enhanced in recent times by an equally deserved reputation for performance and good looks.

Volvo

PV 444, 1948 (5); 122 S, 1964 (1); 760 GLE, 1982 (2); 244 GLT, 1982 (7); 240 DL Estate, 1984 (4); 340 GL Saloon, 1987 (3); 740 GL turbo diesel, 1987 (8).

Saab

The 96 model of 1960s vintage (14 and 15); Saab 9000 (6 and 16); various versions of the 900: turbo (9 and 11), with view of engine compartment (10), and convertible (12).

GERMAN ENGINEERING

MERCEDES

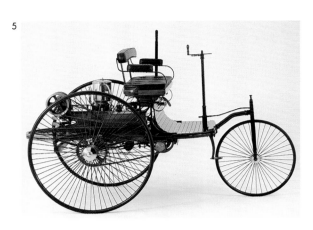

Mercedes typifies the German automobile industry. The story begins with two pioneers, Gottlieb Daimler and Karl Benz, who each made notable advances in the years 1880 to 1890 but failed to capitalize on their early progress. In 1926 they finally joined forces and established an industrial group of which the automotive division, Mercedes, is nowadays but a small part. The first Mercedes was in fact a Daimler belonging to an Austrian businessman. He renamed it Mercedes – after his daughter – in order to take part in a race. This was in 1899. The Mercedes label was initially applied to racing cars; not until 1926 did the first Mercedes-Benz saloon appear: the Stuttgart. This was followed by many other models designed by Ferdinand Porsche: the Mannheim, SS, SSK, and so on. Often incorporating the latest technical developments, Mercedes cars quickly acquired a reputation for robustness, reliability and performance, which they have never lost. This is as true of the impressive official cars, the *Grosser Mercedes* of the 1930s, as of today's striking 600 model; of the legendary 300 SL Papillon sports car of the 1950s as of the contemporary 190.

Throughout the world – in Japan, the United States and Europe, in countries rich and poor – Mercedes is, for many people, the embodiment of perfection in automobile engineering.

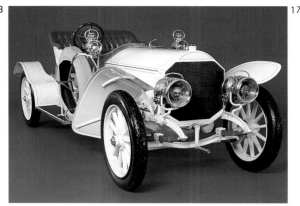

The first Benz: a tricycle, dating from 1884 (5). Benz 35 PS, of 1901 vintage (13); Mercedes-Benz Mannheim, 1926 (3); and a 130 H, dating from 1933 (6).
540 K, 1936 (2).
The Type 170, 1952 (4) and Type 200, 1936 (7).
Benz 28/32 Phaeton, 1904 (8).
A 1935 version of the 500 K (9) and the 540 K (11).
A 1907 Sportswagen (17).
The 300 SL roadster, 1957 (18) and a 190 SL of 1963 (14).
1964 and 1966 models of the 230 SL (10 and 15).
A six-door 600 Pullman (12).
A 1987 version of the 500 (1 and 6).

PREVIOUS PAGES: Porsche 911. Insets, left to right: the 2.8-litre Audi 80 E; a 1927 Mercedes-Benz; and the 1990 version of the Mercedes 300 SL.

OPEL · VOLKSWAGEN

Adam Opel was a successful bicycle manufacturer. On his death in 1895, his widow and five sons decided to convert the family factories at Rüsselsheim to automobile production. The first model, brought out in 1898, was effectively a Lutzmann, and this was followed by French Darracq machines produced under licence. 1902 at last saw the arrival of a true Opel, the twin-cylinder 10/12 PS, the first in a long line of roomy saloons with similar names. But it was the "Doktorwagen", in the second decade of the century, and the "Laubfrosch" – or "tree frog", so named for its green colour – that established the marque's reputation: the Opel was a solid, reliable car at a reasonable price, in return for which the customer expected to forego a certain degree of comfort.

In 1929, with one of the Opel sons concerned mainly to break records in rocket-propelled machines, the marque encountered financial problems. It was bought out by the American group General Motors, which, like Ford, was looking to internationalize its operations. Opel's strategy remained much the same, however, and the Olympia (later the Rekord), Admiral and Kapitan of the 1930s departed not at all from established tradition. The year 1936 was marked by the appearance of the Kadett, the smallest of the Opel range, though certainly not the least famous. The Ascona and the Manta, in the 1970s, and today the Corsa, Omega, Calibra and ever-present Kadett continue to hold high the Opel banner.

For many years **Volkswagen** produced only one model – the Beetle – which proved the most popular car in the world. Not until the early 1970s was there a change of policy, with the introduction of the Golf, the Passat and the Scirocco. These have since been joined by the diminutive Polo, the Jetta and a sports coupé, the Corrado: another shrewd move by Europe's biggest motor car manufacturer.

8

13

17

9

14

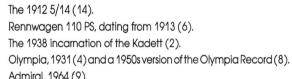

18

10

Opel
15

The 1912 5/14 (14).
Rennwagen 110 PS, dating from 1913 (6).
The 1938 incarnation of the Kadett (2).
Olympia, 1931 (4) and a 1950s version of the Olympia Record (8).
Admiral, 1964 (9).
Rekord, 1972 (11).
Senator Silver, 1986 (13).
Manta GTE Saloon (1).
The 1989 edition of the Kadett (15).
Calibra 2.8l (7).
Corsa GSI (10).
Omega (12).

11

16

Volkswagen

A 1989 example of the Golf (3 and 14).
Jetta GTI (17).
Polo (16 and 18).

12

AUDI • BMW • PORSCHE

Audi, now the jewel in the crown of the Volkswagen group, is a marque with a long history, though at one time it seemed threatened with extinction. In 1909, August Horch, having lost control of the marque bearing his name, set up the rival Audi company ("Horch", in German, means "listen" in English, which translates as "Audi" in Latin). Until 1929, his cars engaged in ruthless competition – on the race track and in the showrooms – with their Horch counterparts. In that year, Audi was absorbed by DKW, whose small cars were then all the rage. During the Depression, in 1932, DKW, Audi, Horch and Wanderer all combined to form Auto-Union; this explains the four-rings symbol which now graces Audi cars. Of the four marques, only Audi was revived when Volkswagen later took control of the group. Audi has since led the way in the development of four-wheel drive [integral transmission]. Its high performance models sell well, deriving prestige from the Quattro's many victories in rallying. With production figures of half a million cars a year, Audi is now a marque to be reckoned with.

Bayerische Motoren Werke, or **BMW**, was founded in 1918 and first concentrated on building aircraft. In 1923 the company entered the field of motorcycle manufacture, then in 1928 turned its attention to automobiles, buying out the firm of Dixi, which had just designed a car of that name. The Dixi was BMW's first great success. Many others followed, in particular the amazing 328, a streamlined sports car of 1930s vintage, and, after the war, the 503 and 507 models. Today, the 3, 5 and 7-series, produced in Munich, are valued around the world for toughness, class and outstanding performance.

Though **Porsche** was established in Stuttgart in 1938, it was not until ten years later that the marque began designing and producing its own models. The company has specialized in luxurious, high-performance sports

coupés, whose rounded forms have remained virtually unchanged over the years. Enjoying an international reputation on a par with such marques as Ferrari and Jaguar, Porsche continues to market the magnificent 911 it first brought out in 1963. Tradition demands it; the car has become part of the Porsche legend.

Audi

Audi 80 turbo diesel SE (15); 90 sport (16); 100 Quattro, with view of interior (17 and 18); Spider (12).

BMW

A series 3 model (7); the 323 cabriolet (8); 518i (13); series 5 engine (9); M 635 csi (11 and 14); 735i (10)).

Porsche

A 356 of 1949 vintage (2); 1979 edition of the 924 (5); 911 Carrera Targa (1); 944, dating from 1988 (3); 959, also 1988 (6); and 928 (4).

MOTOR RACING

THE LE MANS 24-HOUR RACE

Of the many different races in the history of motor sport – from the early road trials of more than a century ago to the modern Grands Prix – there is one whose prestige has never waned, overcoming every crisis and always arousing public interest: the Le Mans 24-hour race. It has been run every year since 1923, apart for an interruption during the war and immediate post-war years (1940-1948), bringing together on the Le Mans circuit the top racing drivers and their machines and an average crowd of 200,000 spectators.

The story begins in 1922, when the trio of Charles Faroux, Georges Durand and Emile Coquille – journalist, general secretary of the Automobile de l'Ouest and industrialist – decided to inaugurate a new type of race, combining speed and endurance to perfection. Since then the race has changed a good deal, the circuit having been modified several times, but the spirit of Le Mans remains inviolate.

The race was contested for the first time on 26 and 27 May 1923 over a 11.01 mile circuit. The unofficial winners were Lagache and Léonard, driving a Chenard-Walker machine, who covered 1,380 miles at an average of 57.54 mph. They head a roll of honour of enormous distinction, which includes such great marques as Bentley (five victories in the 1920s), Alfa Romeo (winners four times in the 1930s), Jaguar (five wins in the post-war years, Ferrari (seven victories in the 1950s and 60s), Ford (four wins in the 1960s) and Porsche (winners no less than eleven times between 1970 and 1986).

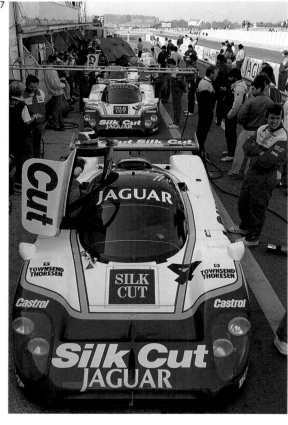

The race has, of course, had its darker moments, as in 1955, when a Mercedes careered off the race track and cut down dozens of spectators in the stands. The difficult circuit, which includes the interminable Mulsamme Straight (where in 1990 a Mercedes reached over 250 mph), has also claimed the lives of many drivers. But despite these accidents, Le Mans is, and always has been, the most prestigious motor race in the world.

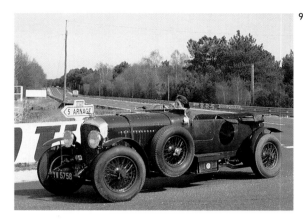

16 The line-up at the start (2).

Jaguar
C Type, 1953 (1); Le Mans Type, 1957 (6); D Type, 1954 (19); 1987 and 1989 entries (7 and 20).

Aston Martin
1955 and 1959 entries (3 and 4).

Alfa Romeo
In 1923, the inaugural year of the race (5).

Ferrari
1960 entry (8), 250 GTO (11) and PS (12).

Bentley
4.5-litre model, 1929 (9) and Speed Six. 1930 (14).

Mercedes
300SL, 1952 (10).

Porsche
1981 entry (13) and 917 competing in 1970 (16).

A view of the 1955 race (15).

Ford
GT40 (17).

Mazda
Mazda, 1991 (18).

PREVIOUS PAGES: the Mercedes-Sauber C9 competing at Le Mans in 1991. Insets, left to right: three 1992 racing cars: McLaren-Honda (F1), Lancia Delta Integrale (Rally racing), and Williams-Renault (F1).

ROAD RACES • RALLYING

In the early years, motor racing – then generally organized on public roads between one town and another – went hand in hand with technical progress and the creation of new marques. In the late nineteenth century and the first half of the twentieth, it was often in competitive situations that important new developments were tried out for the first time. In those days, road races were more than mere speed trials; they tested the strength and reliability of a car to the utmost. In events such as the "international rally towards Monte Carlo" (as it was originally called), the aim was to arrive at one's destination with one's car intact, rather than to drive as fast as possible.

First organized in 1911, the Monte Carlo Rally is typical of the major road events which now count towards the world rallying championship. The cars which have distinguished themselves over the years are household names and have generally achieved success in a far wider context: Hotchkiss in the 1930s and immediate post-war years, Mini-Cooper and Porsche in the 1960s, the Alpine-Renault A 110 and the Lancia Stratos in the 70s and, more recently, the Audi Quattro, Peugeot 205 and Lancia Delta – legendary cars, the standard models of which have sold in large numbers.

Some of the great events have disappeared over the years, as the road networks of industrialized countries have improved. This has been true of the Italian Mille Miglia and other European endurance races. On the other hand, in recent years we have seen the development of exciting new rallies, particularly in Africa, such as the Paris-Dakar event.

An Alfa Romeo competing in the 1930 Mille Miglia event (9).
Sunbeam Alpine, 1950 (5).
Hotchkiss, 1950 (7).
A Lancia Fulvia in the 1971 Monte Carlo Rally (10).
Mini-Cooper (11).
A Fiat 131 Abarth, 1977 (3).
Lancia Stratos (2 and 6).
Alpine A 110 (8).
Audi Quattro, 1983 (12).
Peugeot 205 turbo (13 and 14).
Lancia Delta Integrale, 1989 (4).
Toyota Celica, 1991 (1).

FORMULA 1

Although Grand Prix racing began in the 1920s – with Alfa Romeo winning the first ever constructors' championship in 1925 – it was not until 1950 that the world championship was organized on professional lines in accordance with formula specifications. In the over forty years since then, over five hundred Grand Prix races have been contested around the world, and all the great marques have at some time or other taken up the challenge of Formula 1. In the 1950s, the great Italian Marques reigned supreme: Alfa (1950 and '51), Ferrari (1952, '53, '56 and '58) and Maserati (1957), with a brief Mercedes interlude in 1954 and '55. With the arrival of the 1960s, the British came to the fore: Cooper (1959 and '60), BRM (1962), Lotus (1963, '65 and '68) and Brabham (1966 and '67), though the genius of the legendary Enzo Ferrari – "il Commendatore" – ensured that the Italian marque regularly prevailed in the drivers' championship (1961 and '64, then again in 1975, '77 and '79), to the great joy of the Ferrari *tifosi* – fans.

The 1970s were dominated by the all-powerful Ford Cosworth engine, which brought victory to several different marques: Matra (1969), Lotus (1970, '72 and '78), Tyrell (1971 and '73), McLaren (1974 and '76), Williams (1980 and '82) and Brabham (1981). The year 1981 was a revolutionary one: Renault made its debut in Formula 1 using a turbocharged engine, the superiority of which soon became evident, even though this innovation was not to benefit the French marque which had pioneered it! In the following years, however, it guaranteed the success of BMW-Brabham (1983), Porsche-McLaren (1984, '85 and '86), Honda-Williams (1978) and again McLaren (1988 and '89). Japanese supremacy continued into the post-turbo era with the Honda-engined McLaren (1990 and '91), then in 1992 Renault finally saw the fruits of its technical pioneering, with the help of drivers from the Williams stable.

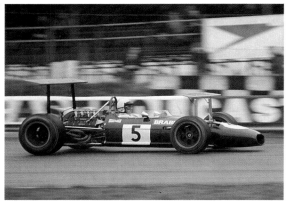

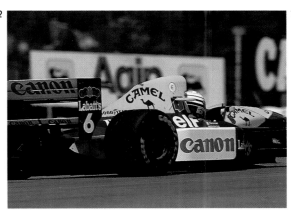

Alfa-Romeo, 1950 (5).
Ferrari, 1951 (8).
Mercedes, 1955 (3).
Maserati, 1957 (11).
BRM, 1962 (14) and 1963 (17).
Lotus, 1965 (16).
Jack Brabham's Repco-Brabham (4 and 9).
Matra, 1969 (6 and 10).
Ferrari, 1975 (7).
Renault, 1982 (1)
Lotus, 1984 (2).
McLaren-Honda, 1989 (13).
Williams-Renault, 1991 (12 and 15).

SOME GREAT RACING CARS

Motor sport has always given constructors – whether the great marques or small-scale enterprises whose sole aim is to design and build prototypes of this kind – the opportunity to experiment with new, original, and often zany ideas in the fields of both mechanical engineering and aerodynamics. This is as true of the early Italian racing cars designed by the likes of Alfa, Fiat and Lancia as of many recent Formula 1 machines. No holds are barred when it comes to designing a racing car. Engineers will think nothing of adding two extra wheels, as in the case of the Matra-Tyrell shown here, or aerofoils, as first tried on Chaparral models at Le Mans. Aerofoils have, of course, since become commonplace, first on other racing cars, then on standard production models.

But it is speed above all that has always drawn participants and spectators to motor racing. The early Alfas were capable of well over 62.5 mph, and it is now not unusual to see Formula 1 cars travelling at speeds in excess of 185 mph (even though, with their ultra-light materials, they weigh an average of only 500 kilos). Looks are important, too. For purists, the accumulation of publicity stickers on the bodywork of racing cars is an abomination. Therefore the decision of a marque like Mercedes never to let its famous "Grey Arrows" be defiled in this way is praiseworthy indeed. Mercedes racing cars have always been models of their kind – jewels of the race track.

Mercedes

The 6-cylinder Rennwagen, 1906 (5); a 1934 type W25 (2); a 1939 W165 model (1); a W196 streamliner of 1954 vintage (6).

Alfa-Romeo

Alfa 8-cylinder machines dating from 1930 and 1932 (15 and 3); Alfa competing in the French Grand Prix, 1924 (12).

A Cadillac racing car (9).
Cars racing at Donnington, 1937 (4).
A 1937 Auto-Union machine (7 and 8).
Fiat 75 hp, 1904 (14), and Fiat's entry for the French Grand Prix of 1922 (16).
McLaren CanAm, 1970 (11).
The six-wheeled Elf-Tyrrell (10).

THE SHAPE OF THINGS TO COME

SPACE WAGONS AND OTHER PEOPLE CARRIERS

When Renault unveiled its Espace model in June 1984 – a revolutionary automobile designed by the engineers, technicians and stylists of the Matra company – it was effectively introducing a new generation of vehicles: the space wagons. While maintaining all the advantages of the traditional saloon in terms of road-holding, performance and manoeuvrability, these cars offered greatly increased interior capacity (seven passengers, or five passengers and a large amount of baggage).

The Espace was extremely compact (shorter in fact than the Renault 21), aerodynamic, and capable of maintaining a high average speed. The success of this new-style car was such that the major manufacturers, particularly the Japanese, quickly followed suit. The Espace was soon joined by the Toyota Previa, the various Mitsubishi Space Wagons, the Nissan Prairie and, from America, the Chevrolet Lumina and the Oldsmobile Silhouette.

In response to the new fashion for roomy, comfortable cars, the Japanese also increased the interior space of their traditional all-terrain vehicles. The influence of the Espace had proved seminal. Meanwhile, the Espace itself continued to evolve, the growing range of models including sporty turbo-charged and four-wheel drive versions.

Renault

Renault Espace (11) model 2000 TSE (3) and its interior (7).

Mercedes

Mercedes GE 300 4WD (1) and short wheelbase version (4).

Toyota

Land Cruiser (2 and 6), Previa (5) and Space Cruiser (13).

Mitsubishi

Space Wagon (9), Space Runner (10) and Shogun V6 (8 and 14).

New-look London taxi (12).

PREVIOUS PAGES: Concept Car Silver Blue. Insets (top to bottom): the Renault Espace, and a 1990 Vauxhall prototype.

CONCEPT CARS

One of the most exciting developments of recent years has been the appearance of large numbers of concept cars: experimental prototypes designed by the major manufacturers. Although there is only the slimmest chance that we shall ever drive one of these machines, they give us a glimpse of what cars might be like in the 21st century. Since the late 1980s, the most amazing prototypes have been exhibited at Tokyo, Geneva, Detroit, Paris and other major Motor Shows. Typical is the [Laguna], a fully reversible two-seater unveiled by the Renault stylists in the autumn of 1990. Equally bold in conception are such models as the Toyota FX, the Pontiac Pursuit, the MG EXEE, or the Peugeot GX JA.

Japanese manufacturers have gone even further. Leaving aside Mazda's suitcase-car, which is something of a gimmick, the major Japanese marques are all working feverishly on prototypes, which before long may well result in mass-produced models. These include cars with the accent on the vertical for crowded urban traffic conditions, cars with extendable bodies, and cars with a high degree of computer control. No stone is being left unturned by modern engineers.

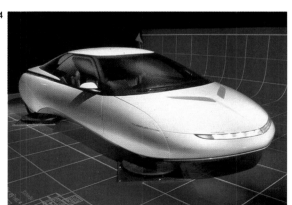

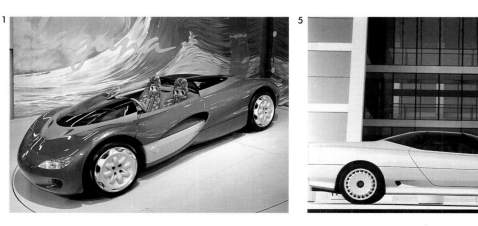

Renault Laguna 1990 prototype (1).
A futuristic Vauxhall 1988 (2).
Vauxhall SRV, 1970 (12).
Toyota FX V2 Concept, 1988 (3).
Pontiac Pursuit (4).
MG EXEE experimental car (5 and 9).
Futuristic Design Car (6), proto design (18).
Mitsubishi 1988 NEC Motorshow concept car, 1988 (7).
On-board computers (8 and 19), navigation system (13).
Aztec 1988 (10).
Eco 2 concept (11).
Chevrolet Express (14).
The Sinclair C5 battery-powered cycle (15)
The Bond Bug (16)
Suzuki COS III, 1988 (17).
Peugeot GXJA, 1988 (20).
BMW Isetta (21).

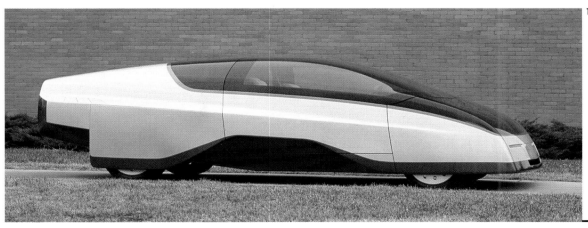

INDEX

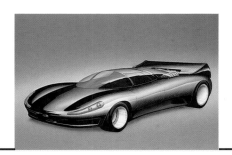

INDEX

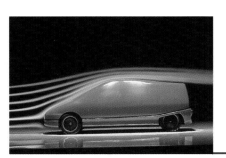

PHOTOGRAPHIC CREDITS

The publishers wish to thank the following organizations for their kind permission to
reproduce the photographs in this book:
The National Motor Museum, Beaulieu, England; Quadrant;
Jaguar; Dupé; Fiat; Lancia; Alfa Romeo; Daimler-Benz Archives;
Mitsubishi; Landcruiser; Toyota; BMW; BMW GB; Ligier;
Mercedes Benz France; Citroën; Rover Group; and Gamma, Paris.

Produced by Copyright-Studio for Colour Library Books
Translated from the French by Simon Knight in association with
First Edition Translations Ltd, Cambridge, UK
Layout: Jacques Hennaux
Montage: Catherine Bataille
Picture research: Image Select, Patricia Coupart
with the kind assistance of Alexis Goldberg, Image Select, London